dinner WITH *Muhammad*

A SURPRISING LOOK AT A BEAUTIFUL FRIENDSHIP

MARILYN HICKEY

FRANKLIN GREEN
PUBLISHING

Dɪɴɴᴇʀ ᴡɪᴛʜ Mᴜʜᴀᴍᴍᴀᴅ
Published by Franklin Green Publishing
P.O. Box 51
Lebanon, Tennessee 37088
www.franklingreenpublishing.com

ISBN 978-1-93-648723-3

Printed in the United States of America
10 9 8 7 6 5 4 3 2 1

To Reece and Sarah Bowling—for their unending love and years of support and encouragement to pursue my calling to "Cover the Earth With the Word."

contents

FOREWORD

By Imam Mohammad Ali Elahi
Founder, Islamic House of Wisdom, Dearborn, Michigan

Marilyn Hickey, Stephen Kiser, and some members of Marilyn's ministry visited our Islamic House of Wisdom in June 2009. Marilyn and I performed an interfaith prayer for a mixed Muslim-Christian audience gathered at our mosque. The service was concluded with a Lebanese style dinner in the reception hall of our center.

What really impressed me most was Marilyn's faith, sincerity, and willingness to reach out and serve people through prayer and blessing. In that prayer service she asked the Almighty to heal the sick and bless them with health and happiness. Our interfaith prayer service was enjoyed by both Muslims and Christians because of so many similarities both in words and the spirit.

Prayer is a big part of our faith; it is part of our daily practice. Prayer helps us to replace our fear with faith, stress with peace, weakness with strength, and negativity with positive energy. Even in the worst, most stressful moments of our lives, when we call God with His beautiful names and qualities, we get energized and feel great hope and healing.

The Lord is identified in the Quran with so many beautiful names, including: The Guide, Gracious, Guardian, Merciful, Magnificent, Majestic, Holy, Helper, Peace, Forgiving, Friendly, Provider, Protector, Patient, Omniscient, Omnipotent, All Hearing, All Seeing, Grateful, Generous, Just, Benevolent, Wise, Loving, Witness, Truth, Trustee, Praiseworthy, First, Last, Light, King, Kind, Unity, Unique. Prayer is a bridge that connects us to the center of all these qualities and provides us with all the power we need to fix our relationship with our Lord, our family, and humanity.

I remember Marilyn saying we must do our part and He will do His. When we yield our will to God's will, He enacts His Will in our lives. Our will plus His power produces true willpower!

Another important point in that prayer service and dinner was that we both emphasized that faith without good actions has no fruit. The real devotion is to discover the truth and share it with your intention, expression, and action. In addition to God's glorification, I mentioned some other commonalities between Muslims and Christians. I remembered Adam for his knowledge and repentance; Noah for his patience and perseverance; Abraham for his determination and submission; Moses for his courage, commitment, and struggle; Jesus for his purity, love, and sacrifice; and Muhammad for his wisdom, mercy, and integrity.

Yes there are differences between Muslims and Christians in some characteristics of our belief systems, but so many disagreements exists among Muslims themselves and Christians themselves! The Crusaders decided to destroy those with whom they disagreed. We must make dialogue over our disagreements and agree to disagree over certain issues and leave the Lord to judge the areas of our disagreement on the day of resurrection.

It was God's desire for us to experience this diversity and struggle to choose the straight path. He could have created us to be identical, but out of His wisdom He gave us the gift of diversity, so enjoy the fruit of our challenge in search for the best.

It's through openness, tolerance, respect, and dialogue that we can build the bridges of understanding and cooperation and bring peace, prosperity, freedom, justice, health, and happiness for all. We need to continue to pray together, work together, and struggle together to remove the roots of ignorance, poverty, racism, war, violence, and terrorism from our world.

Our prayer session in 2009 was humble in size, yet it was an absolutely pure and sincere step in that direction and destination. Amen!

INTRODUCTION

Dinner with Muhammad is a very important book for me because I believe it will open the hearts of people all over the world to pray for Muslims rather than hating them. We are to show the love of God to this group of people that comprises one-fifth of the world's population.

In this book I share the personal experiences I've had with Muslims on a one-on-one basis in my own city. I have them over for dinner, they take me to lunch, I have Bible studies with them, and several of them now come to my church. It is really a blessing to reach out to a people who I think are sometimes shocked by us.

Muslims are very open to prayer, and even though they usually know nothing about the Bible, they revere it as a holy book. Anytime I get the chance to say to a Muslim, "May I pray for you in the name of Jesus?" I consider it a wonderful opportunity. They love prayer and they certainly love prayer in the name of Jesus. I believe this book will shock you as to how much favor you can have with Muslims in your own city. It will also encourage you to pray for Muslims around the world.

This book also introduces ways to build bridges of communication and not burn them. Many books on the market contain warnings about the dangers of Islam. I believe these books are factual and maybe even necessary, but the purpose of my book is to get you involved in building bridges.

Some of the greatest things I've seen are miracles of healing in the name of Jesus. Muslims are extremely open to believing in the healing power of Jesus because it states in the Qu'ran that Jesus heals the sick. This has proven to be a big key and a wonderful tool to build bridges with Muslims. It has also been key when sharing Jesus with Hindus, Buddhists, and atheists.

Dinner with Muhammad will put a new passion in your heart to extend the love of Jesus toward those that we believe have abused us. But the reality is that they live in our cities, in our towns, and maybe even in the house next door. What can we do? How can we build a bridge and not burn a bridge? This book will open your mind and your heart in a new way to express the love of Jesus.

dinner
WITH
Muhammad

Part I

I

tea with a muslim widow

~~~~~~~~~~~~~~~~~~~~~~~~~~~~~~~~~~~~~~~

Do not fear mistakes. You will know failure. Continue to reach out.

—BENJAMIN FRANKLIN

It was October 6, 1981, and the day began peacefully with a blazing-blue sky, perfect for a military parade in Cairo, Egypt. Citizens gathered to celebrate Armed Forces Day, but more than that, Anwar Sadat and the majority of Egyptian citizens were celebrating peace. Abruptly, the pageantry ended when three men hurled grenades from out of the mob. Machine-gun fire gushed into the spectator stands, turning patriotic cheers into shrieks of terror. President Sadat had been assassinated by the Brotherhood, a group of Islamic radicals that is also linked to 9/11. While this beloved leader, a symbol of peace, stood at attention, bullets pelted through his body, leaving him fatally wounded. Twenty others were killed, and four American diplomats were injured. Once again, Egypt was reeling.

This well-respected president's legacy was brutally attacked by Muslim terrorists who felt he compromised Sharia Law—that under Sadat's administration Islamic law was not given precedence. Despite the outbreaks of violence in the previous months between Christians and Muslims, this was to be a day set aside to commemorate the goal that Egypt was striving toward—peace.

But Egyptian Muslim radicals opposed Sadat's landmark peace treaty with Israel and hoped to impose Islamic rule in Egypt. I remember those shocking moments after his death was announced, when President Reagan poignantly addressed the nation:

> Today, the people of the United States join with the people of Egypt and all those who long for a better world in mourning the death of Anwar Sadat. President Sadat was a courageous man whose vision and wisdom brought nations and people together. In a world filled with hatred, he was a man of hope. In a world trapped in the animosities of the past, he was a man of foresight, a man who sought to improve a world tormented by malice and pettiness. As an Egyptian patriot, he helped create the revolutionary movement that freed his nation. As a political leader, he sought to free his people from hatred and war. And as a soldier, he was unafraid to fight. But most important, he was a humanitarian unafraid to make peace. His courage and skill reaped a harvest of life for his nation and for the world. Anwar Sadat was admired and loved by the people of America. His death today—an act of infamy, cowardly infamy—fills us with horror. America has lost a close friend; the world has lost a great statesman; and mankind has lost a champion of peace. Nancy and I feel that we have lost a close and dear friend; and we send our heartfelt sympathy to Mrs. Sadat, to his children, who were here such a short time ago. Thank you very much.

For weeks, you couldn't turn on the news without hearing about outbreaks of violence in the slums of Cairo and tensions rising between Christians and Muslims, each group blaming the other for the hate crimes and violence. Thousands of suspected terrorists were rounded up and jailed in the following weeks, leaving Egypt in a more devastating state of fragmentation. Tragically, Anwar Sadat's quest for peace ended in heartbreak and bloodshed, forever altering the life of the First Lady of Egypt, Jehan Sadat. My heart went out to this brave widow from the East who I admired from my Western world.

I knew of Jehan's important efforts in the 1960s and 1970s that clearly established her humanitarian heart. There was her work with Egypt's civil rights—often called "Jehan's Laws"—which granted women a variety of new rights, including those to alimony and custody of children in the event of divorce. She founded Wafa'Wa Amal (Faith and Hope) Rehabilitation Center, which assisted disabled war veterans with rehabilitation services, helping those who are often marginalized and destitute in society. As an advocate for Egyptian women, she played a vital role in the Talla Society, a cooperative in the Nile Delta that assists women in becoming self-sufficient. Her patronage toward the Society of Cancer Patients and the Egyptian Blood Bank and her work with orphans all revealed how her caring hands reached out to the suffering. As I reflected on her dedication to her husband, her country, and her people, I felt challenged and in awe. *Surely, God, I can give more, reach more, too, with your help.* Never had I dreamed that a year later the remarkable Jehan Sadat would invite me to tea—all because of a foolish mistake I had made.

A few months after Sadat's assassination, I received a call from a consultant asking if I would help bring Bibles translated into Arabic to Egypt and air a satellite program from Cairo. The timing seemed right in the wake of devastation, and I saw it as an opportunity I'd been praying for, to reach more people in need of hope. After some meeting and planning with my international team, we decided to do a satellite broadcast right out of Cairo; it would air in twenty-nine cities to raise funds for the Bibles. Providentially, I found a technician in New York who agreed to help us and who was willing to travel there on short notice. Everything fell into place rather quickly. Officials told me I needed to bring $5,000 to Cairo for the taping and to air the program.

Stepping off the plane, I was preoccupied with thoughts of how all this was going to come together—we were actually going to reach a Muslim audience, and I knew a lot could go wrong. Before I hailed our taxi, I stood at the curb quietly and breathed in Cairo, a city infused with a lingering sense of history. The noisy, overcrowded streets interrupted my thoughts and drew me into this exotic city. We merged into the maze of traffic, and my cab driver leaned on his horn, only allowing him to roll the cab a few inches closer to the stoplight with no regard for a particular lane of traffic. "Sorry for the traffic!" he politely shouted toward the back seat.

I rolled the window down so I could enjoy the sights a bit more. The hot spring winds were blowing dust around and the warm air was sooty, reeking of *ma'assil,* a kind of tobacco that smells like incense. Local fare was being prepared on kitchen carts up and down the winding streets, enticing tourists with fresh bread and fava beans mashed with lemon, oil, and cumin. A licorice juice vendor chanted, "This is a wonder! Sweets from wood!" I wanted to stop and experience the people, but I knew I had to go straight to the Egyptian government if this was ever going to happen.

The cab driver dropped me in front of a generic, white-brick government building. Through a ticket window, I said, "Sir, I'm here to do a satellite program here in Cairo." I listed the names of all those on the travel team. Adhering to what they had requested, I gave them the money, signed the papers, and considered it a done deal. I then headed to the hotel and gathered our team so we could get started.

Everyone had made it over from the States by now and had checked in. "Okay, let's get this taping done. I paid the government, so we are free to get going," I began.

"You gave them the money? [*Sigh.*] You'll never see it again. You should have never paid the government," said our technician. "The taping won't ever happen now."

"What?" I sat there stunned for a while, unsure what to think. Surely this couldn't be true.

I had no idea that our money was not safe with the government officials. I couldn't believe it—the money was considered to be gone. I knew we had to try to get help immediately. I remembered the gift I had brought for Manasat Kamal, a Christian in the Egyptian parliament. A mutual friend in the States had asked me to deliver a copy of the Bible on tape for him. Remembering the gift, I called, thinking he might be able to help, and asked if he could come to the Hilton. He agreed.

"Marilyn, so nice to see you in Cairo! May I ask what brings you here?"

I told him the dilemma we were in, and he concurred with my technician. "How foolish could you be? You should have never given the money to the government. You will not get to air your program! Well, let me make a phone call. I have a friend, Ms. Sadat. She may be willing to help you."

The next thing I knew, Manasat's brother was driving me to Jehan Sadat's mansion on the Nile River. She graciously invited me over for tea, and I knew this was the kind of networking only the Lord could do. I'm not sure how much Manasat shared with Jehan, if she was supportive of our efforts, or what she knew before I arrived, but I tried to remain patient and hopeful during the lengthy security check. Phone calls, exchanging passport information, background questions, and calls back to the United States consumed the hours; finally, after what seemed to be a chain of days, we were told I could go see her.

The mansion was elegant, full of English flair. Jehan's mother was British, and her heritage was apparent in the décor. The foyer swelled with a mother's pride, displaying a handsome picture of Jehan's son, who was dressed in his military uniform. "Welcome to Cairo, Marilyn." I could see kindness in her almond-shaped eyes, which revealed her father's Egyptian heritage. She was charming, but reserved. She wore a deep violet suit that looked stunning on her, and I admired how it looked against her auburn hair. Cordially, she led me into the parlor.

"Marilyn, tell me, why are you here?" There was not much small talk at first. She wanted for us to clearly establish the point of my visit.

"Well, I'd like to air a satellite program in twenty-nine cities, and I brought a crew to help me record them. The government asked me for the money first and—"

"Oh, my," she interrupted, "well, everyone knows you should never give the money first to the government," she teased in a serious tone.

"Ms. Sadat, I've already done it."

She paused as her butler came in to place the tea service on the table. "How could you be so foolish? [*Sigh*.] Well, let me make a phone call."

She went to another room, leaving me with my regrets. *How could I have been so foolish?*

After several minutes, Jehan came to tell me where I should go to tape the programs. I didn't have any idea what strings she had to pull for us, but she gave me clear instructions to follow and told us to move quickly. I felt overwhelmed with gratitude and somewhat taken aback that she went to this trouble, particularly after I discerned in our short conversation together that she was still grieving over the passing of her much-adored husband. Though we had just met, I wanted to show my sensitivity toward her loss, so before we departed I asked her if I could pray for her; graciously, she said, "Yes."

Quickly, we checked out of our hotel, and we made sure we left nothing behind with our name on it. We drove in the dark to the studio, feeling our way through the streets and back alleys of Cairo around ten o'clock at night, which made the whole thing seem all the more foreign and obscure. The facility, looking nothing like a recording studio, was crude and dirty, with cats running all around scrounging for food. I got over that quickly, determined to remain focused so the taping could get done. I shared a short message of encouragement and expressed our desire to share God's Word with the people of Egypt. It was a very simple message, as it needed to be, so that we could all get out of the country before morning. After the final take, we immediately left the studio to catch our flight home.

My time with Jehan Sedat took a little less than an hour, and God did exponentially more than I could have anticipated. The First Lady spoke to me with authority and offered solutions in the midst of her own pain. We talked some about her hope for better opportunities for women in Egypt and her efforts to bring about equality. We talked about the joys of being a mother, about family, and about God. And through the swift changes in direction of our conversation, consistently her eyes reflected back kindness and empathy as she poured milk into our teacups. I was deeply moved by her hospitality and her warm handshake as we said goodbye.

Clearly, it was the Lord's wisdom that orchestrated the events of the day, nothing I could have even hoped or tried to do myself. Jehan's actions revealed to me that she believed a Muslim and a Christian could sit down, have tea, and build bridges. And that my Christian prayers were welcomed. I respected the torch for

Egypt she carried in honor of her late husband—whose dream was now *her* dream: Peace. Her humanitarian heart reached out to me, and God was growing something inside of me that I didn't fully understand. And this opportunity came all because of my mistake with the money. This brief encounter, you could say, was the beginning of a greater understanding of "love your neighbor as yourself"—even if the neighbor is Muslim.

2

gaza within reach

*For Gaza shall be forsaken, And Ashkelon desolate;
They shall drive out Ashdod at noonday, And Ekron shall be
uprooted.*

—Zephaniah 2:4 NKJV

Small Reaches

I love Egypt. Back in 1998, my husband Wallace and I decided to take a special vacation, just to enjoy its beauty. Hosting countless tours of the Holy Land, many evenings I've witnessed the sun setting over the Pyramids, turning the sand to gold. Egypt was a playground of adventure for my children, Michael and Sarah. Camel rides. Tranquil boat tours down the Nile, hosted by a captain who wore his free-flowing, colorful *Jalabia*—very different seafaring garb than that worn by our Western navigators. For years, this country has captivated my heart.

I had just finished an extended stint with a fast-paced schedule and cheerfully anticipated some rest, time to breathe in the beauty of Cairo. We boarded in business class, situating ourselves for the long flight. Just as I was about to rest my head back, my leg brushed up against the *burkha* of a Muslim woman, and through her veil I heard sobbing. She made her way up to first class, and I noticed a limp in her walk. My spirit became very unsettled, and I sensed a strong prompting to pray for her. But I kept telling myself, "You're on vacation, relax." I also reasoned, "She is in first class; you're not supposed to go up there anyway." But the Lord was speaking to me: "I want you to go pray for her." I told Him, "Lord, I can't go into first class." He replied back, "Do you love them?"

With conviction, I made my way up to her seat and knelt down. "Excuse me, I noticed you are in pain. May I pray for you?" Without hesitation, she said, "No problem; yes, thank you." The burden lifted as I asked God for His healing hand to touch her. I thanked God for His love for her and for nudging me to reach out.

I would call such occurrences God moments—how Muslims have entered my life. And through very ordinary situations, I have learned to be obedient when the Lord is asking me to share compassion. The natural inclination to reach out, to celebrate people and culture, was traceable in my formative years. But I never set my sights on ministry. I had no idea where God was going to take me just by stepping through small, random acts of faith.

Gaza City, 2009

The city was now under the oppressive rule of Hamas (*Harakat al-Muqawamat al-Islamiyyah*, meaning "Islamic Resistance Movement"); it was a miracle we even got in for two hours. The Israelis were instrumental in allowing us to get beyond the borders, and we knew we had to take advantage of any window of hospitality, no matter how small, to build future opportunities. I knew that one of the leaders in Hamas had a recent conversion experience and became a Christian, so I knew it might result in a opening a door into this imprisoned city.

Gaza is hell. Every day, over one million people wake up to the harsh war of poverty in their city. The average citizen is forbidden to cross the border. Jerusalem is just a stone's throw away, but the people cannot visit to benefit from the resources. The borders are locked down. Endless food lines fill the streets with starving people. Seventy percent are unemployed and under the age of twenty-five. Muslims, Christians, Jews, and atheists grow up together in bondage to an unjust regime. Everyone is crying out for freedom. Young people have such bleak futures with little guarantee of safety.

Stephen Kiser, who sets up all our international contacts before we hold an event, had been working to find opportunities in Gaza, knowing I had a desire to go. I had just finished hosting a tour in Israel, and after the group had departed we decided to stay and try to cross the border. After many phone calls with our friends in Jerusalem and the Israeli Mossad, who are equivalent to our Secret Service, we weren't sure if it was going to happen even up until the night before. Finally, Stephen got the call that he was allowed to go in, but I was not. This didn't sit well with me—I just knew God wanted me to go with Stephen—but I also knew our friends and Stephen had done all they could to do. I trusted and waited. And finally that morning, to the astonishment of everyone, I received clearance. Though we had been to countless Muslim countries, we didn't know what to expect—so few Westerners had ever dared to enter. We were ordered to walk through the checkpoints alone, so Stephen went in first.

As I entered the desolate border and approached the gated checkpoint, dust whirled ahead of me for what seemed to be endless desert miles. This bombed-out, war-torn city was in physical and spiritual ruin. All I could see was the barren road ahead, so I thought about the beautiful faces of the people of Gaza who bore the image of God and deserved to have a future. I must have walked well over a mile before I spotted a building. Here, security again interrogated me: "Why are you here?" "Do you love Israel?" "Who do you know?" I waited for clearance. The various checkpoints felt like walking through a federal prison, but there were no voices or signs of life. I went through more doors to find nothing on the other side and started to feel very disoriented. The barbed-wire fences outside the building confined my view. Stephen, several checkpoints ahead, called me on his cell and let me know what to expect, thank God. Had I not had his prompts cautioning me along the way to brace myself, I'm not sure I would have had the courage to keep going. We were completely cut off from the modern world and the taste of freedom felt like a million miles away. I had to remind myself to breathe. To keep walking.

Security directed me toward a small shack, where Stephen had already arrived. Here, we met with two leaders; one was Muslim, and the other was Greek Orthodox—the Archdiocese of Tiberias and patriarchal representative for Gaza. Every moment mattered, so we quickly huddled in as they poured the tea. And then all the feelings of terror left me. Our Western and Eastern cultures coalesced, and the threatening atmosphere subsided. In that austere, cramped space, we all became aware of our common limitations as human beings.

"*¿Cómo puedo ayudarte?*" ["What can I do to help?"] They knew we came to offer humanitarian aid. The Muslim leader, to my surprise, understood Spanish better than English, so that's what we spoke.

"*Nuestros jovenes necessitan trabajos y entrenamiento,*" ["Our young people need jobs and training,"] said the Muslim leader, who came to represent an openness to Christianity.

The two leaders concurred, "Please come back and bring the help we need."

Though it was an amicable meeting, the forceful urgency for us to get out of Gaza by 4:00 p.m. pushed us along because of Hamas intimidation; we knew we were about two miles from the border of Israel. We went through the same process on the way out. Camera surveillance. Passport check. Turnstiles that were locked down and didn't allow you to pass through. Everything was bound up. As I entered the elevator, a robotic voice instructed me to push the button to the third floor, only to find no one there. "Wave your passport," an anonymous security voice instructed. We knew we were being watched from all possible directions, and we knew Hamas could kill us.

Despite the brevity of our meeting, I knew the Lord had orchestrated this two-hour stop after our Israel trip, though I don't fully know where it will lead in the future. God is always doing more than we know. A phone call here, a Christian leader there, favor with ambassadors—all were a part of this formidable miracle. And with His help, I believe that God is going to allow me to go back, to share the hope I have and what resources He may give me. I don't know how I'll be able to do it, but the leaders specifically asked me to help provide jobs for young people—that's now a dream growing in me. I want to return to Gaza with tangible resources that will help build trust. Because Hamas continues to refuse to recognize the state of Israel, it continues to occupy a crippling economic hole. But as strange, dangerous, or foolish as it sounds, I desire to meet with Hamas and build relationships with some of the leaders. In just those short moments we were there, we were able to determine the greatest needs of the people and to gain an inside perspective of Gaza.

For me to even understand this, I have to look at the life of Jesus. He hung out with the marginalized in society—tax collectors and prostitutes, the despised and the "unclean." In light of 9/11, it is understandable how we can justify our suspicion of Muslims. We all want a safe country. Yet I also know that Jesus' worldview always sets my own belief system upside down. In Jesus' time, a tax collector was viewed much as we would view a terrorist or a pedophile today—unworthy of mercy, incapable of repentance. Even a beggar wouldn't take money from a tax collector. No one wanted to be associated with him. Yet Jesus chose Matthew, a tax collector, to be a disciple. And He invited himself to be a guest at Zacchaeus's house (Luke 19) and announced it publicly. Deeply moved by Jesus' unashamed display of acceptance and love, Zacchaeus repented of his acts of corruption and vowed to offer restitution to his victims. And then he threw a feast for them.

I'm certain God's heart is for the people of Gaza, which is why I'm willing to sully myself and befriend the marginalized. I can't say I set out intentionally to build relationships with Muslim nations. Rather, it has been a process—a process I'm still walking through when opportunities arise. Sometimes it means walking through walls of steel; sometimes it means looking around to see who is next to me on an airplane. Clearly, it's the path God has paved for me over the past few decades. I've been to almost every impoverished nation in the world, and never have I seen people live in a world so depleted of hope as in Gaza. From my life experience, I know that Jesus heals. I want the people there to encounter wellness and wholeness as a result of my organizing a gathering where no one is turned away.

Historical Tensions

The clash between Muslims and Christians has been present for fourteen centuries. Living in the twenty-first century, we are aware of the growing tensions presented because of the war on terrorism. The Christian faith centers around following Jesus Christ. The Muslim faith centers around the prophet Muhammad. Christianity spread rapidly right after Jesus' resurrection and ascension. Many first century believers were martyred for their faith, and the early church rose up in strength through the work of the disciples and Paul's missionary journeys. Throughout the book of Acts, the disciples are moving in the power of the Holy Spirit, preaching the Gospel and establishing His church.

Through persecution, hardships, and martyrdom, the Roman Empire was evangelized. By the end of the fourth century, Rome was declared a Christian state.

Muhammad, born in Mecca, which is now present-day Saudia Arabia, claimed to have a vision in 610 AD. The angel Gabriel gave him messages from God; those messages are now called the Qu'ran. His teachings weren't accepted in Mecca, so in 622 he traveled to Medina and settled there. During these initial years, the movement became not only a religion but a social and political crusade. Muslims view Muhammad as the successor to Jesus and claim that the teachings of the Qu'ran remain undefiled.

When you compare Muhammad's teachings with the teachings of Jesus, they differ a great deal. Muhammad is known as a warrior who conquered by the sword. The Qur'an teaches, "Slay the idolaters wherever you find them . . . lie in ambush everywhere for them. If they repent and take to prayer and render the alms levy, allow them to go their way . . ." (Sura 9:5). Jesus, in contrast, lived as a servant, meek and gentle. He spread a message of forgiveness, repentance, and serving others.

The claim that Muhammad became more prominent than Jesus is one of the reasons Christians cannot move away from the real tension—that you have to deny the deity of Jesus Christ, His resurrection, and the gift of salvation in order to embrace the teachings of Muhammad. Islam and Christianity have been at odds since Muhammad began spreading his teachings. The teachings of Muhammad and the teachings of Jesus are very different. Muhammad pursued his faith through violence and raids. Jesus, on the other hand, taught His followers to pursue peace, to love the enemy, and to bless those who curse you.

The remarkable speed of Islam's religious expansion came through military conquest. Mohammed converted Arabs to Islam with the promise of salvation for those who died fighting for Islam and the lure of fortune for those who succeeded in conquest. The caravan raids of the early years of Islam soon became full-scale wars, and empires and nations bowed to the power of this new religion.

To study the Christian Crusades gives the reality of how deep the wounds are between these two world religions, and even to bring them up in relation to the war on terrorism is controversial. But to acknowledge the bloodshed, the great divide that has existed for over fourteen centuries, is important in understanding the unspoken tension the world carries. Christian historians acknowledge the political elements that played into the Crusades, but for the most part they believe that participation in the wars came from a defensive positioning. When Muhammad was waging war against Mecca, Christianity was the dominant faith with the most wealth. For Muhammad, there was no tolerance of Christianity; he came to destroy with the sword. Because of Christianity's prominence, Christians were the prime target for those engaged in these holy wars, though at the time anyone against Islam was to be slain. By the eighth century, Muslim armies had conquered all of Christian North Africa and Spain. Islam captured two-thirds of the old Christian world, and the Crusades were a response to the seizing of religious freedom. When Crusaders did capture a Muslim area, the Muslim residents were still free to practice their religion. For the Christian Crusader, the goal was religious freedom, not forced conversion.

The crimes and brutality of the Crusades are undeniable. Some became more wealthy, but to crusade was costly, so most lost wealth. The belief in fighting for religious freedom far outweighed the motive to collect plunder. With no chain of command or sophisticated strategy, the Crusades continued on, the first century being the most successful. War is always full of injustices. Whether you admire the Crusades or not, the world today wouldn't exist as we know it without them. The Crusades spanned from 1098 to 1291. And these religious tensions have influenced fourteen centuries of hostile conflict, as we see the tensions rising in the very same places of conquest centuries ago. To follow the literal teaching of Muhammad means to war against anyone who doesn't embrace Islam, but not all Muslims follow the Qu'ran to that level. Yes, Hamas does, which is why I continue to marvel at how God let us get inside the borders of Gaza.

We can't ignore the history; understanding the root of the tensions gives us an idea why the issues are so complex and still remain. The Muslim religion came to the United States through the slave trade in the 1800s, mostly from Muslin regions in West Africa. A trickle of Muslim immigrants began arriving around 1840, mostly those desiring to prosper and then return to their homeland. In the 1930s, the Black Muslim Movement brought religious and racial tensions to the forefront. The beliefs were based on Islamic teaching and black supremacy. The hostilities grew from African Americans who felt they lost their Muslim identity through the slave trade and racial segregation. The Nation of Islam (NOI), formed in 1930, was the largest organized form of Islam in America. It labeled white people as "devils." Malcolm X became the most famous leader of this movement, which promoted complete segregation. The Nation of Islam went through various leaders and reforms throughout the mid to late twentieth century and organized the Million Man March in 1995. Today, the group is more inclusive to other races; however, it is still viewed as a hate group by some civil rights organizations.

The two events of the last fifty years that have had the greatest impact on the modern Islamic world are the re-establishment of the state of Israel in 1948 (desired by Muslims throughout history and viewed as holy) and the Iranian revolution. The seizure of the American embassy and the holding of hostages under

Khomeini in the 1980s showed the conflict of a Muslim revolution once again.

Before terrorist attacks, before we even knew about al-Qaeda and the Taliban, Islam was frequently in the headlines through the late twentieth century and the turn of this century. There were Civil wars in Africa and tensions between Hindus and Muslims in India. Israeli-Palestine conflicts increased, and tensions mounted between Iraq and the United States. Globally, the world became more aware of the unrest in the Middle East that was now impacting the United States.

The devastation of September 11, 2001, understandably caused confusion and stereotyping to increase in the United States. The truth is that stereotyping can keep us from seeing one another as human beings. The extremist groups associated with bin Laden did not represent the majority of American Muslims, but in the aftermath of such permeating evil, relationships were severed and distrust began to run through the fiber of our society. Prior to 9/11, most Muslims worshipped peacefully in their mosques, rejecting the extremist views of the radicals. But Ground Zero left us in a state of distrust and shock. How does a country heal from such an attack?

For me, it still comes down to God's commandment: "Love the Lord your God with all your heart, soul, and mind, and love your neighbor as yourself." And loving a neighbor often means loving someone who believes something different than me. No one has to resolve the historical tensions in order to reach out to a fellow human being, who may very well extend a hand of friendship.

Prayerfully, I wait for relationships to cultivate so that we can return soon. The struggling people are a part of me now—a part of the human race who have dignity but have been robbed of everything else. I know it is hard for people to understand why I extend my hand to hostile regimes, why I bother to try to build relationships in a post-9/11 world. And yet, I know I'm to continue to reach out with compassion. Despite the dangers and the voices of critics, Jesus compels me. I continue to pray. Seek. Wait. Knock. And the doors continue to open, some small and some much bigger than I dreamed.

How did it all start for me? I have to say it began in a child's heart.

3

my formative years: sovereignly, I tripped into this

For we are God's handiwork, created in Christ Jesus to do good works, which God prepared in advance for us to do.

—EPHESIANS 2:10

Pittsburgh, 1941

When I smell the comfort of hot, homemade bread in the oven, I think of my childhood friend, Clorinda Flora, from Italy—the first friend I had from a foreign country. We met during the brutality of World War II. During those years, my dad built warships for the military, which took us to Pennsylvania for a time. The community where we lived was somewhat clique-ish, and I experienced a good bit of snobbery; perhaps this is why even now I'm always inclined to cheer for the underdog.

I was aware as a child of what it felt like to be in the unpopular crowd. Clorinda, too, felt left out, like an outsider, maybe being so far from her homeland—though there were other Italian families around. I felt drawn to Clorinda, so when my aunt told me she had invited the whole Flora family over for spaghetti, I knew we were destined to be friends.

"Ciao, Marilyn. Mi chiamo Clorinda." I thought she spoke in the most beautiful language I had ever heard. I liked that we were so different.

Stylish fashion and famous artists. Exquisite spices and pastries. She'd tell me how she missed the deep, greenish-blue glow of the Mediterranean Sea. Clorinda brought another dimension to my childhood, as she let me breathe in another part of the world, away from a raging war. I think she taught me the beauty of diversity at a very young age, during a time when prejudices dictated the slaughtering of millions of Jews. Our friendship grew throughout elementary school, and so did my love for foreign languages—and my determination to see the world.

1943, School Days: Lessons in Determination

During my last year in Pittsburgh, I met my Latin teacher, Dr. Hawes. His pedagogy was the challenge I needed, but I didn't understand the strategy at first—its ability to motivate me. As a graduate of Yale, he esteemed the writings of Cicero and Caesar, and he loved the game of chess. When exam days came up, he'd pull out his chess pieces and play until every student finished, muttering and chuckling at his own wit. Dr. Hawes became my favorite teacher, but not initially. He motivated students through intimidation—and in my case, it worked.

"Marilyn, go to the board and conjugate, 'to love.'"

I approached the board quietly, a bit numb with fear. I grabbed the chalk, trying to muster up some confidence to remember: case, number, gender. I attempted to conjugate—*amo, amas, amat*. Well, my work went all wrong, and he let the whole class know of his disapproval. I walked back to my desk humiliated, just sobbing. I kept my head down until the bell rang, which seemed liked eternity to me. I gathered up my books, eager to make a quick escape from Dr. Hawes.

"Marilyn, please come to my desk. You know, I'm hard on you because you can do better. I must warn you, my bark is much bigger than my bite. So no more tears. Very well, carry on."

After Dr. Hawes showed me mercy and a bit of his heart, I

went out of my way to do well in his class. His pedagogical fear tactic began to work on me. To my surprise, his influence on my life led me to take five more years of Latin.

Denver, Colorado, 1946

As a young girl, I used to intently watch the planes fly overhead, full of wonder. How could they just float up there? Where were they going? What kind of people were on the planes? The desire to travel began for me at a very early age, but it wasn't until I turned sixteen that I actually took my first flight—from Denver to Pittsburgh to visit my favorite aunt, Aunt Ethel. Going to see my aunt let me dream well beyond Pennsylvania, and I couldn't believe I had a ticket! Aunt Ethel had no children, so she had a way of making you feel like you were the most important person in her life. She loved people, and people loved her in return. Her lavish generosity to those in need allowed me to see what beauty really was, beauty that went well beyond her peaceful blue eyes and striking dark hair. I watched her tend to the sick at the nearby hospital and admired the way her kind but firm words kept the patients going and holding on to hope.

"Aunt Ethel, I want to be a foreign ambassador."

"Marilyn, you can be whatever you want, and God has given you a strong mind. I want you to memorize all your declensions and conjugate until you can do it backwards. It will pay off." I never questioned her belief in me, and she never said anything that led me to believe women had to have smaller ambitions.

I knew my dreams were safe with Aunt Ethel in Pittsburgh and that there was room in our relationship for me share even bigger dreams along the way.

In middle school, high school, and college I went on to study French and Spanish—I loved the romance languages—and I even took Greek. Thoughts of other cultures, and of adventures overseas, were always with me. I graduated from UNC in Greeley, Colorado, in 1953, where I majored in foreign languages and minored in English. I had a knack for languages, but it was more than that: I knew there were people to meet behind the languages, and that is where the adventure was—with people. Now I felt ready to jet-set around the world on the way to becoming a foreign ambassador. But then, the Lord proved to have other plans.

Bigger Faith and Bigger Dreams

My mother was an Irish-French woman, born and bred in Texoma—who had faith as big as Texas. I grew up with Methodist roots, but more on the liberal side of the denomination. I don't remember hearing much about the Bible in our church growing up; yet God had a firm hand on my family.

While my father provided for us and we always had food and shelter, he struggled with a mental illness, which led him to be violent toward my mother at times. Mother kept us all going, encouraging us, and provided the stability my brother David and I needed.

The Lord became more real to me when I witnessed His power right in my home. I must have been around nineteen years old when my mom started going to a charismatic church—very different from our Methodist upbringing. I didn't care for it much, but I didn't complain about it. My mom occasionally asked me to come with her on Sundays, and I thought the people at the church were way too emotional and way too loud. I didn't like hearing people speaking in tongues and all the emotional overtones left me skeptical about all of their noisy worship. But during this time, I noticed Mother had a new confidence about her faith, which my father also noticed. He hated her new church and became more verbally abusive the more involved she became.

"Mary, if you go to that church one more time, I'll kill you!" he hissed. But Mother continued to go faithfully, despite his disapproval. Then the day came that I feared most.

"Marilyn, where is your mother?"

I knew she was at church, but I replied back to my father, "I don't know," trying to look as unruffled as possible. A couple of hours later, Mom came home, and he grabbed a knife as he heard her come in the back door.

"Have you been at church?" he intoned with the knife poised.

"—In the name of Jesus, you drop that knife!"

I saw my father shrink to the floor, completely overpowered by the Spirit. I witnessed with my own eyes the power of God protect my mom. Peace flooded the room. I knew my father couldn't harm her, and my fear ceased.

"John, I will continue to be a good wife, cook, clean, and do your laundry. But I will also continue to go to church three times a week."

My father remained on his knees for quite a while, though I'm not sure how long. I had never witnessed anything like that before, but I knew I had witnessed God's power in our home. He became more relevant to me, more traceable even in the small things, after that encounter.

A Dream About the Future

I started to go to church on a regular basis, but quite frankly, my main motivation was meeting my social needs. I attended, still pursuing what I wanted for my life, not considering that God's ideas might be different. Not too long after the confrontation I witnessed between my parents, I met Wallace Hickey at church. I hadn't met anyone quite like him before. On our first date, he was quite frank with me: "I've served the devil with all my heart; I've served God with all my heart. I'm not going to marry a woman who is half-hearted in her walk with God."

His faith pierced my heart, and I told him I'd pray for a deeper encounter with the Lord, though I already had committed my life to Christ at a Methodist youth camp at age sixteen. I knew these few days now set aside for prayer weren't just about Wallace or a future husband. They had to be about me and God. That night, the Lord came to me in a dream and told me, "I have something so wonderful for your life, you can't imagine." At that moment, I surrendered my own dreams and followed God's lead.

On December 26, 1954, I married Wallace Hickey. But before I did, I wanted to be sure of one thing. "Wallace," I asked, "you aren't going to be a minister or anything like that, right? I don't have any desire to be a minister's wife."

At the time, Wallace worked for a successful recording label in Denver and did well as a businessman, so I was pretty certain I knew the answer. I also had settled into teaching foreign languages and loved the serendipity that happened every day in the classroom. He honestly answered, "No, not that I know of." His answer left me at peace, and I didn't worry about being confined to a small, local church, with no hopes of experiencing other cultures. So my hopes were high that I'd still be able to explore the world and travel. I loved serving our church, and we were active members—we sang in the choir, and we taught Sunday school. But I had no ambition to go further down the road in ministry. None whatsoever.

Three years into our marriage, Wallace discerned through prayer that the Lord was calling him to be a pastor. Astonished, I knew I couldn't fight this or I'd be fighting against God. I, too, moved forward, away from what I wanted, asking God to lead me as well. I remembered back to what he spoke to me in the dream, "I have something so wonderful for your life." We ended up moving to Amarillo, Texas, where we accepted the positions of associate pastors.

At first I hated it and wanted to go home. I felt trapped in the small, dirty, parsonage that felt so crowded for the two of us—let alone the mice and cockroaches.

"Wallace, we are not living here; I want to go back to Denver."

"We're staying! I'm not going to let a house keep us from serving the Lord."

And so, we stayed until our next assignment. I'm ashamed of my initial attitude but grateful my husband saw the importance of the people there. He recognized God's hand on us before I could.

Realizing the Dream

Over the years, I've been to more than twenty Muslim countries—including Morroco, Lebanon, Syria, Ethiopia, Sudan, Indonesia, and Malaysia—and in all my travels, I never felt put down for what I was doing or for being a woman. My travels have allowed me to be the recipient of extravagant hospitality and a guest at some of the most enticing dinner tables. Sure, there are always critics, suspiciously wondering, "Why are you dining with such sinners?" But the Lord has shown me why I should and has granted me favor to visit places that have typically been considered off limits to Christians. God's plan for my life has always proved to be better than what I could dream on my own. He used Mr. Hawes to set determination in my heart, so maybe one day I would have the courage to cross formidable borders. And He used Aunt Ethel, and her belief in me, to push me toward how much God believed in me. And then, at the right time, Wallace pushed me to make God bigger in my life and I began to give God parts of me that I held onto selfishly. Through all my school years, my sights were set on being a foreign ambassador, and all the while the Lord was grooming me to be an ambassador for Christ. And yes, I sort of tripped into His dream for me.

"Do not despise these small beginnings, for the Lord rejoices to see the work begin" (Zechariah 4:10a NLT).

4

circle around the sun

Go, swift messengers! Take a message to a tall, smooth-skinned people, who are feared far and wide for their conquests and destruction, and whose land is divided by rivers.

—ISAIAH 18:2 NLT

Khartoum, Sudan, 1997

Sudan is a paradox, a place of oppression at the hand of Muslim extremists, yet also a land where envoys have been sent down the Nile to Jerusalem, carrying diplomats. To the ancient Egyptians, Sudan was known as Cush, the source of ivory, gold, incense, ebony, and slaves. The book of Acts describes a meeting between Philip and a royal eunuch from the Land of Cush, Ethiopia, who was returning home after his pilgrimage to Jerusalem. Cush is a city that lies between the Blue and White Nile, where it gets the meaning of its name, "end of an elephant's trunk." Many scholars have suggested the Garden of Eden is in this region of the Blue Nile. Once again, God opened a marvelous door for us after we spent a great deal of time in prayer, fasting, and contacting key leaders who could help us.

Getting into Khartoum set a new precedent for our ministry team in reaching out to Muslim countries. God paved the way at the right time. In 1997, our ministry team hosted a five-night healing meeting in Khartoum, Sudan. Bishop Adier, who represented all the church leadership, had the connections in government that were necessary for us. Though this meeting took place in a pre-9/11 world, the hostility between Christians and Muslims was fierce and alive. The modern civil wars between Southern and Northern Sudan have taken thousands of lives and continue today. We knew this event meant risk, but all of the team involved came to trust God for protection and the doors that opened were opened because of His favor upon us.

Sudan was the homeland of the refugees known as the Lost Boys, who fled from extremists from Northern Sudan between 1983 and 2005. Approximately twenty thousand boys as young as four years old made the trek to Ethiopia to escape from their targeted villages. To not run meant falling into the hands of a militia in which boys were forced to serve as Muslim combatants. Without food, water, or knowledge of other African countries surrounding the area, the boys had no idea of how long the trek to safety might be—no one knew what loomed ahead. The unforgiving wilderness caused thousands to fall victim to fatal diseases, starvation, and wild animal attacks.

Some migrants landed in Khartoum, looking for work and schooling. As we stepped out onto the streets of Khartoum, my team felt the scars of war as we brushed up against the crowded city. The historical divisions made the people vulnerable to all kinds of attacks, both physical and spiritual. One of Satan's biggest lies throughout the world is to make us believe we are all enemies. Satan's name means "one who casts something between two things to cause a separation." In all my travels, I find this to be true. People are more the same than different. We all want to be able to take care of our families, to have work, to be loved, and to find meaning in life.

Khartoum has strong Christian roots that lead back to the

Old Testament. Also present in the culture is Sudan Animism, a tribal religion believing spiritual beings interact with humanity, either helping or harming them. But most Sudanese are Muslim. And in the midst of the real tension, we were there to build a bridge, despite Satan's plot all along—to separate and divide people from God and one another.

As a mother, I naturally questioned if my daughter Sarah should be a part of this event, but God led us in the decision and Sarah did not have children at the time, which factored in my letting her come in with me. Sarah and her brother Michael traveled with Wally and me throughout their childhood, and she saw the fierce friction between Jews and Muslims, and Christians and Muslims in the Middle East. We traveled regularly to the Holy Land as a family, so early on Sarah knew what religious tension actually felt like. At just five years old, her first up-close interaction with an Arab happened.

During a ministry tour through Egypt, Sarah somehow found herself locked inside a bathroom stall on the second story of a restaurant with a big group of people. Over the toilet, Sarah noticed a window. She climbed up to see if she might find help, but instead she saw an armed Arab man looking up at her, positioning his machine gun in a turret. It's one thing to see soldiers or militia on the news as a child, but it's quite another to walk on the streets with them. It's something she has never forgotten.

As we got out of the taxi, Sarah leaned over and let out an intense whisper, "Mom, I'm scared out of my skull! . . . But I know I'm to be here." The media covered the event on TV, so that anchored us a bit and provided a measure of safety too. We stayed close together, mindful that we did have enemies who did not want the event to happen. But we kept trusting and believing that God's protection surrounded us.

Because of its stronghold of extremist Muslims, Sudan has been described as "where Satan sits." Yet our hearts were full of expectation and love for the people of Sudan. We provided ministry training for the Christian Sudanese, and leaders came from surrounding countries, despite the spiritual conflict. To be able to encourage these Christians made every obstacle seem insignificant. Gratitude swelled up in their hearts toward us and we couldn't have felt any more love from these hospitable Sudanese than if we were among lifelong friends back at home.

The April sun burned down on us as we gathered and shielded the attendees with a small tent cover. The intense heat gave those on the platform no relief, but the Sudanese didn't even notice the sweltering air. God's favor beamed down on us like in the words of Isaiah, "This is what the LORD says to me: 'I will remain quiet and will look on from my dwelling place, like shimmering heat in the sunshine, like a cloud of dew in the heat of harvest.'"

During one of the first morning sessions, I began teaching on Jesus' miracles, and I noticed the crowd started pointing at the sun, and then screaming and shouts swelled. I asked the translator what they were saying. "Jesus is in the sun!" he exclaimed. African ululating rose up among the crude bleachers, "Ul-lul-lul-lul-lul!" I've heard this jubilant sound many, many times over the years, and I don't think any other sound captures God's joy over His people so well. The African ululating grew louder and louder. Some said the sun pulsated and flashed, and others said that they saw a likeness of Jesus in the sky. A dark ring appeared around the sun, and people began to run toward it, compelled to see the miracle in the sky. During this amazing sight, more than a thousand came forward to receive salvation. The ring continued to show up during the following afternoon sessions. Everyone saw it repeatedly—I don't know how many witnesses.

Why did God choose to do a miracle in the sky? I don't fully understand, but I do know such a miracle cannot be orchestrated by man or any event. Before we had left for our trip, a team member of ours had told Sarah about his daughter's dream, in which she saw circles around the sun. He wasn't sure what to make of it, but he felt compelled to share it with Sarah right after his daughter told him about it. As we gathered that night for prayer, the team member told all of us about his daughter's dream. Perhaps it was to build up our faith in what only God can do. Maybe it was to show God's authority over the people of Sudan and His rule over the expanse of the sky. Maybe the prayers of a faith-filled man like Joshua were answered, similar to Joshua 10 when God caused the sun to stand still so the Israelites' enemies could be defeated. Whatever the reason, we knew the Holy Spirit was at work in ways we didn't anticipate, and it isn't possible to understand all the ways a sovereign God chooses to move. So we kept on believing Him to bless the event and show us His favor. Each day the crowd grew from ten thousand to tens of thousands. They came to hear about a healing Jesus.

Sarah and I love to pray over the people, and we formed a prayer tunnel with our team, to be able to touch them and pray over those who desired prayer. Each day attracted more and more people. Though the masses came, God gave us specific opportunities to touch people individually with God's generosity. We had received word that a disabled woman wanted to come for healing. We arranged for a taxi to bring her to the meeting and she came with great expectancy. This precious woman received God's healing touch and didn't need a taxi home—she walked. The miracles were breathtaking and glorious. To see stretchers being carried home empty and crutches left on the platform pushed out the oppressive hot breeze, filling us with the fresh awareness of God.

The African attendees responded with deep joy and emotion. I continued teaching about Jesus' miracles because I knew that many didn't know the Bible well and they didn't have many re-sources. The stories of healing in the Bible left them amazed and hungry for more understanding of what God can do. Every time we gathered, I preached a simple gospel message. One man who had been blind for three years came up to testify. A deaf boy received hearing. Tumors disappeared. Testimony after testimony, God's healing touch was undeniable. Hundreds of thousands were impacted by the love of Jesus Christ.

Divine Protection

President Al-Bashir didn't know me personally, and I never met him, but he was fully aware of our presence in the country and was concerned enough for me at this event to arrange our trans-portation in his bullet-proof private limousine. His office helped provide all the security we needed. After our last afternoon event, some government officials asked us to report to Al-Bashir's palace. Frankly, I wondered if we were in some kind of trouble, aware that he was one of the top ten dictators of the world at that time. The five or six of us who went to the palace felt at ease to learn that our hosts spoke English and invited us for tea. To our amazement, we were asked to come back to do humanitarian ef-forts. I boldly asked, "Could we show the Jesus film?" They agreed.

Before leaving, I took an afternoon to go into the Ethiopian refugee camps located in Khartoum, where there are masses of tents erected, just barely standing up in the desert sun. As I walked among them, words weren't necessary to grasp the injus-tices in their stories. You can see the terror in their eyes and how they carry themselves. Over half the world's refugees are women—orphaned, widowed, divorced, abused, victims of exile and abandonment. Studies show that women refugees actually experience more violation of human rights than men and they are much less likely to have a say in their future. Proverbs 31:8

came to mind as I prayed and walked the grounds, "Speak up for those who cannot speak for themselves, for the rights of all who are destitute."

As soon as we left, I wanted to go back. The liberties God provided for us to reach out to the people left us astounded. Not once did I feel hindered to pray for the sick. I thanked God for the miracles we witnessed, the physical and spiritual healing, the ring around the sun, and particularly for the biggest miracle of all—getting us there. I fervently prayed, "Oh God, please let us come back to these people."

Khartoum, Sudan, 2007

It took ten years for all the doors to open back up and for God to answer that prayer. Through genocides, civil wars, and terrorism, we continued to pray, "God, please let us back in." Our world had to recover from 9/11 and we knew it wouldn't be easy, but around 2004 the urge to build more relationships and go back intensified in me. My team pressed through obstacle after obstacle, and after three years of prayer and fasting, relationship building, and hard work, the second event we dreamed about became a reality.

Stephen Kiser, our global ministries director, believes this indeed is his vocational calling. I don't think anyone can do it without a deep conviction to persevere through all the red tape, slammed doors, and setbacks. Every Muslim country poses different dynamics and winding roads to conquer. So faith in God and in only what He can do is essential.

It took Stephen time to gain the trust and support we needed to proceed with a healing event and training school. God required us to believe He could do it, but even when we believe and exercise our trust in God, the fact remains it's intimidating. Even when you put a deposit down on a venue or secure dates on a calendar, at a moment's notice it can all change due to governmental control. Stephen's wife and daughter understand why he does what he does. They tell him, "I know you are taking Jesus to those in need."

The December 2007 Khartoum event defined a lot for all of us, what we were willing to do and risk, what it meant to love an intensely Islamic region that historically has persecuted Christians. And you do think, *Well, if it is my time to die, then it's my time.* But time is a gift from God, and so when you offer Him your time, He fills it with good things when we are willing to take a risk for another soul. In the midst of dealing with our doubts, God once again proved to be faithful.

First, our efforts started in Washington, D.C., which later down the road connected us, once again, with officials of Al-Bashir's office. Stephen's efforts began with building a relationship with the Sudanese ambassador over tea in D.C. Then he began to travel to Sudan, where he spent many months prior to our healing event in the homes of Sudanese people who had big hearts. When you spend time with families and hear what is in their hearts and learn their struggles, the cultural gaps are forgotten and what you are left to deal with is a person created in the image of God. Stephen continued to meet with ambassadors and leadership, learning how they viewed him, if they trusted him enough to allow us to come. In the course of three years, Stephen had to prove to the leadership that he only desired to bring blessing to the country, not harm. Not an easy thing to accomplish when the foundation of a culture has been shattered by genocide.

Like Ethiopia, Sudan's Christian heritage goes back to the early centuries of Christianity. All of the Christian churches work together. Coptic, Anglican, Catholic, they all believe there is one enemy: Islam. Most oppressed countries desire some form of democracy, and the same is true of the religious minority of Christians in Sudan. Having the right political and religious leaders involved is what allows our team to get in.

I take as few people as possible with me because of the reality of danger. I knew about the scares Stephen encountered, so we wanted to make sure all who went felt at peace about it. Sudan's doors were not easy to open, and the best posture to take was to let God lead Stephen as he met officials and gained trust. And through it all, we had to trust His perfect timing, not force something to happen out of mere ambition.

A deeply troubling confrontation happened prior to the event. Two men approached Stephen outside of his hotel and knocked him down as he walked on the sidewalk, a sidewalk typically occupied by ambassadors from all over the world and considered to be safe. About twenty minutes later, someone started pounding on the glass door and shouting, "Go home! We don't want you here!" The hotel window faced an alley, and the men continued to harass him: "We know who you are . . . If you don't leave we will take care of you!"

Stephen reported the incident to the general manager of the hotel, who confirmed how unusual this was. Taking proper measures, the staff watched the surveillance camera to try to identify the two men, but the video footage didn't capture a clear image of them. Police arrived to guard Stephen's door. This happened to be the same day that Osama bin Laden released his video stating that all Westerners were not welcome. When I heard about the threats of the unidentified men, I pleaded, "Stephen, just come home." None of us had gone through anything like that before, and I sure didn't expect him to stay.

"Marilyn, we all know God has sent me here—and I'm going to stay. I really believe God is going to take care of me," Stephen reasoned. "My wife is praying, everyone is praying. I sense a strong peace as I've prayed about what to do, and I'm staying because these people need to know about the freedom of Christ." Though the harassment shook Stephen up for a bit, along with our team back at home, his resolve to stay became stronger and stronger.

God instilled a love for different cultures in Stephen as a child, much as He did me. Stephen found himself thinking through his formative years, "Someday I'm going to help the poor and visit many nations." As he approached college, he continued to be fascinated by missionary reports and God's work in other countries, but he decided to study architecture and then take his wealth to those in need. After completing several semesters of coursework, Stephen attended a revival meeting. He wanted more of God but didn't know what that looked like, but he offered God to lead him wherever He wanted. Years later, while working in Christian TV, Stephen received a vision from God one night in bed. His eyes were wide open, and illuminated on the ceiling were the words, "on the way." Then he fell back to sleep. God continued to speak: *I haven't called you to go on the way through the nations preaching the word. You will deliver finances and send relief. You will help all people of all religions and different groups discover Jesus.*

Later, it all started to make sense. While Stephen served in upper management with Walt Disney World, God had opened all kinds of doors so that he could minister to the employees, sharing his faith. He knew this was part of his training for what was next. Promotions kept coming, and every time Stephen felt like he kept moving closer and closer to the Mouse, questioning God's plan in all of it. He continued to trust and press into prayer. He and his wife, DeDee, found themselves in Denver in 1997, and they came to one of our church services. Pastor Wally mentioned the miracle God did regarding our barrenness. This ministered to DeDee and Stephen in a timely and personal way, as they struggled with the same issue. God later did a miracle and gave them their daughter, Olivia. He knew that those words he had seen on the wall years prior, "on the way," would be fulfilled in global ministries.

The term *humanitarian* took on a whole other meaning for

Stephen when he joined our team. His faith pushed us forward to link arms with the unapproachable. Stephen pressed on with a flurry of meetings with dignitaries and leaders, building trust, though visible progress was slow. Doors opened and doors shut. Finding the balance between gaining political favor and favor among church leaders takes patience, and sometimes it seems like an event hinges on finding one key person.

The first time Stephen went into Sudan, I told him, "Find Bishop Adier—if you find him, everything will be a go." Stephen searched and searched for the bishop with no success. None of it played out like we had hoped. Finally, after Stephen had exhausted all leads, one contact recommended talking to a certain pastor, who might help us locate him. Stephen followed up and found out that Bishop Adier had fallen out of favor with the churches and had begun siding with the government. Conflict between the churches and the government caused him to lose favor with churches due to his financial gain. He fell out of good graces even with his own denomination.

With no connection to high government officials in place, Stephen had to face ground zero. It looked like our success depended on one man, one resource, but it didn't. Psalm 20:68 reminded us where our faith should be: "Some trust in chariots and some in horses, but we trust in the name of the LORD our God" (ESV). The months ahead were all about building trust, though the religious barriers and political red tape seemed to reject Stephen's extended hand over and over. But hope grew in the dark and another connection rose up. You don't know what door will open or close but finally, somehow, Stephen connected with a cabinet member of the parliament who was a Christian and a childhood friend of Al-Bashir.

"Stephen, when Dr. Hickey came in 1997, I remember the circle around the sun. I was there! We want her to come back. You will have favor with the palace," he promised. God is resourceful when He does miracles, and to think that miracle was remembered and opening doors ten years later felt like another miracle altogether. Though we didn't fully understand the circles around the sun ten years ago, we knew that God was still using it for His glory.

Later, we connected with a prominent bishop of the Anglican church, a man whose church had been targeted and bombed. This bishop ended up being the right connection for us, as Stephen mentioned his name to the groups in lower government who didn't know of our organization. His name gave us credibility, and they began to listen to our desire to reach out to Christians and Muslims in Sudan. For us, this proved to be one huge turnkey, and this bishop sent a message to the palace on our behalf. The government, just as it had in 1997, supported me. God formed this inner sanctum of relationships just for us to be able to get in.

The Christians there say they have one enemy—Islam. Yet our favor continues to grow and grow in the parliament. A lot can change in a day; a friend can turn into an enemy. The first bishop I thought was essential for us, Bishop Adier, came back into the picture and knew we now had great favor, but he turned on us and began working against us. His ambitions changed; he now disapproved of us, so much so that he tried to shut down our event our first night because he wasn't chairing it.

Three hours before the event, we received word that Bishop Adier had shut the doors on us. We weren't sure what to do and asked the officials in the stadium, "Is this true?"

"Yes, it's true. If it doesn't shut down, it's an act of God," they all confirmed. The mid-government had turned on us, and at the time we knew about other political tensions, massive demonstrations in the streets. Providentially, this served as a distraction and didn't have to anything to do with us, but God used it so that the attention moved away from our event.

We did still have government police with us and headed to the stadium. It's strange to say, but we arrived there like all was going to go as planned. There is no other way to walk but as His Word says, "walk by faith and not by sight," even down to the minute. When we arrived, we realized that our favor outranked the bishop's mid-level leadership. Al-Bashir's vice president showed up at the meeting, and he took care of the bishop. After further meetings and negotiations, I reached the platform with the approval to speak. Amazed. "Greetings! I want to thank your government and President Al-Bashir for the opportunity to bless Christians and Muslims tonight!"

Could all the Christians be knocked out of Sudan? I suppose so, but officials do want to promote an image of democracy. With that, there is a measure of limited tolerance. If you were to ask a Sudanese, "Can you worship the way you desire?" He or she very well might say, "Oh, yes," but not elaborate on the persecution that may follow. Christian churches are being bombed, children are kidnapped, and such tragedies are commonplace occurrences. As a Christian, it isn't at all easy to survive there, and most evangelists from the States end up leaving. After each event, our prayer is that when we leave the people don't suffer for participating.

I'm grateful for Stephen's calling on his life. He knows this isn't about vocational pursuit but rather about following God. Yes, he has had incredible favor, but it is also mixed with discouraging encounters. Not everyone approves of his presence when he comes to set up an event in a Muslim country. Stephen doesn't hide behind body guards and flashy cars. He goes to the poor villages, talks to the people, some of whom are for and some radically against any Western mentality. But this is how he gets to know the hearts and mindset of the people, engaging in conversation and extending a warm handshake, though he may not receive one in return.

Recently, Stephen took a trip to Greece to do more work in our global ministry's efforts. He'd been working very hard on the Pakistan event and needed time to retreat, away from politics and the weighty issues still pending. On the way back, he stopped in Florida to spend time with his mother. During their time together, she said, "Stephen, you're living your dream, aren't you?"

He answered, "I guess I am, Mother. In some ways it is right on; and some ways it's so different than I'd thought it would be."

Sometimes, we need to step back and evaluate where we are, where we are headed, and why. Stephen shared with me the story of a time when he was flying out of Sudan across the ocean. Trying to get our ministry into Sudan had left him angry, tired, and discouraged. He told God, "I've done as you've asked and given up time with my family, and I'm just so exhausted." Then God reminded him, "What are the blessings you have?" And then He started taking Stephen through his life, back to when he was a child. God showed him the Hand that faithfully had been with him through a tough childhood, an abusive, alcoholic father who served time in prison. God affirmed, "I have brought you through all of that. Now you are going to the nations, ambassadors, kings, and presidents. Look at the favor I have placed on your head." Stephen thought about his time with the king of Jordan and laughed, "What am I doing with a king?" I believe God gives Stephen favor because he is surrendered to this strange paradox of loving both friend and enemy.

It is definitely a mixed bag when you walk alongside the people. Some are shocked that Stephen would even come into their oppressive villages. Others despise his presence, right down to his style of dress. And many buy into terrorism, or at least are afraid to admit they don't, living in the shadows of violence. Some have shouted out to Stephen, "I want you dead!" And then, ironically, even those who believe in Jihad can turn out to be friendly and kind.

As you move among the villages, you see the dry, dirty conditions. Dust is everywhere, even in the nicest places. People survive, but they don't prosper.

But Stephen continues to go because, like me, he believes that they all deserve to know about God's love. And we will continue to go as long as He continues to tell us to go. After two events in Khartoum, ten years apart, we recognize these events to be spiritual signposts, for the people of Sudan and for us. We know it is the work of God, and He calls us saying, "Watch me! See what I will do!"

5

a healing bridge

*And he has committed to us the message of reconciliation.
We are therefore Christ's ambassadors, as though God were
making his appeal through us. We implore you on Christ's
behalf: Be reconciled to God.*

—2 Corinthians 5:19–20

Bridges are everywhere. A trail of stones through a river, or a
fallen log covering the width of a stream can be discovered on
just about every mountain hike. Creation produces them in the
natural rhythm of God's rule. Humanity has been building
bridges since the beginning of civilization, following nature's
declaration for the need to build and connect. God made a bridge
for Moses and His people out of the bottom of the Red Sea. He
built another bridge at the bottom of the Jordan River for Joshua
when the Israelites needed to cross over to safety.

Our Creator also uses people as bridges. Joseph served his father, Jacob, and his brothers during the famine, which gave him
favor with the Egyptians, connecting two disparate cultures—
poor shepherds with wealthy rulers of a thriving culture.
Joshua's assignment meant moving the tribes of Israel into
Canaan, though the land was inhabited by giants. Jesus, the ultimate example of a human bridge, stood in the gap for our sin, so
we can be reconciled to our Father. He wants us to be bridge

builders too. Getting to the other side of where He is leading us to go often takes creativity, patience, and God's help. A bridge can bring the most diverse people to the same place.

Over the years through ministry travels, I've witnessed suffering and pain close up. Poverty and lack of education breed cultural ills that can devastate a nation. The needs of people in Muslim countries are endless. Scripture teaches us that poverty has three causes: natural disasters, oppression of government, and moral failures. Because of the lack of medical help available, the passion to pray for the sick overwhelms me. I believe Christians are to carry a common burden, and that is to pray for those who need healing. No matter where you live in this world, we cannot escape the impact of sickness and disease on infants, young children, young adults, and the aging. An estimated 40 percent of the world's population lacks sanitation, which can lead to all sorts of diseases, diseases carried through unclean water supply. Preventable illnesses here in America are deadly in impoverished nations because most lack access to affordable medicine. While humanitarian aid efforts continue, it is still not enough. Prayer itself is a bridge that transcends miles, and it was through prayer that I realized my neighbor really was someone I've never met around the other side of the globe.

Back in the 1980s, I saw Freda Lindsay, humanitarian and founder of Christ for the Nations International (CFNI), pray over the world. Her love for all people was evident in her life work with CFNI, as well as in her missionary efforts. I figured if she made time to do that, so could I. It took me about an hour to pray and get to every country, and some of the African countries were difficult to keep up with due to names changing, but I wanted to get a sense of where all the countries were and kept with it. Through this exercise, I began to notice how my heart was drawn toward certain countries: Egypt, Morocco, Sudan, Kenya, and East Africa. Although I didn't really recognize it at the time, these were all Muslim countries. I believe God cultivated something in my heart through that season of prayer that has led me to what I do now. Prayer is a powerful bridge and prayer indeed leads to healing.

Healing isn't reserved for faith healers or the spiritual elite. No matter what church I've visited, just about every denomination, the sentiment often seems to be, "God isn't going to listen to a small prayer said by an ordinary person." Yet Scripture shows us that that is not true. The disciples were ordinary as can be—fishermen and tax collectors. God used simple prayers said by simple men to heal the sick in Jesus' name. In Luke 10, the disciples came back and joyfully reported to him, "Lord, even the demons obey us when we use your name!" And Jesus told them, "Yes, I have given you authority over all the power of the enemy and you can walk among snakes and scorpions and crush them." God is calling all of us to pray for one another's healing and to exercise our faith on behalf of one another. Our prayers are a bridge that God uses. Our faith for another can be a catalyst in taking someone to the other side, out of harm's way. We are called to stand in the gap for one another. If we aren't doing it for our brothers and sisters in Christ, then it will be even harder to reach out to those who do not know Him.

I believe we are living in a time when humanity is hoping to witness God's healing power. Agnostics, Muslims, even atheists want to know there is an all-powerful God who loves people from every nation. And healing is something only Jesus Christ can do. Christians believe that, but they often wrongly believe that Jesus will only heal Christians. Throughout His earthly ministry, He reached out to those who didn't know He was the Messiah. Often, He did ask them to exercise faith in God that He'd hear them and heal them.

When I teach in Muslim countries, I've noticed that the people are hungry for prayer—they believe in its power. Prayers for healing are the cry of the heart and the bridge God uses to enter into a relationship. John 5 is a story I often share at healing meetings—the story of the lame man at the Pool of Bethseda. This man lived with paralysis for thirty-eight years and the illness had become a way of life. His situation looked hopeless. This is true for many in Muslim countries. When they are sick, they accept it as a lifelong condition because most do not have the money to receive medical help. I tell them how Jesus loves to heal all people, as they gather in the thousands to hear about the Jesus who heals.

Friends, I love to travel to Muslim countries because Jesus loves Muslims, and so do I. Do you know that I've seen Him heal thousands of people in Hindu countries? And I've seen Him heal thousands in Muslim countries. I've even seen Him heal atheists! He heals those who have never heard the name of Jesus and what He can do! Now, it isn't me, it's Jesus who heals, so let's lift up our hands and believe He can do a miracle for you. The Word of God says He heals, and it says faith comes by hearing the Word of God. Okay, so now you have heard the truth about Jesus, the Healer. Though there are thousands of you gathered here tonight, Jesus sees each one of you individually and He knows what kind of healing you need. When Jesus saw the lame man, He saw all of those gathered at this pool, the lame, the blind, and the deaf. People gathered here believing there were special healing powers in the pool. Well, Jesus saw the man lying there and spoke to him, "Would you like to get well?" He replied, "I can't, sir, I don't have anyone who can put me into the pool." Jesus told him, "Stand up and pick up your mat." So Jesus was asking Him to trust and exercise His faith. So lift your hands in faith and say, "I believe you, Jesus." And then the next thing Jesus asked him to do was walk and then instantly the man was healed! He rolled up his mat and started walking. So check, examine yourself. Do you see any manifestation of healing? Sometimes it is gradual, sometimes it is instant. Praise God for what He is doing! I know many of you are experiencing a miracle right now.

Their response back always boggles my mind. There's no manipulation or coercion involved. Muslims willingly come to pray with me, and I boldly pray in Jesus' name. The Lord is faithful and performs more miracles through such simple prayers because they indeed believe me when I tell them Jesus heals. And that creates an environment where miracles really do happen. The atmosphere is charged with faith.

This is a powerful bridge; really, prayer is a bridge we have with believers and nonbelievers. Everyone needs prayers. There are people in this world who haven't experienced the blessing of someone praying for them. I think when God does a healing in your life, it is hard to not share it with others. I've experienced physical and spiritual healing in my life, and I know Jesus as my Healer.

God's healing power can heal us instantly. When I was thirty-four years old, I found a mass on my breast. I prayed for healing and miraculously within twenty-four hours it vanished. But sometimes God's healing comes through a process.

When I was twenty-three years old, the doctors told me I couldn't bear children. My husband, Wally, and I tried going to different specialists and the answer didn't change. My condition was genetic; my aunt had suffered with the same struggles with infertility. But Wally always believed God was going to open my womb, and I do believe there is great power in the healing prayers said by a husband.

Years later we attended an event in Dallas, Voice of Healing, to hear an evangelist. Wally and I were not in ministry yet; we went because of our hunger for God. We didn't go seeking healing for me, but the evangelist called me out of the crowd and I had the most unusual experience with God. The Holy Spirit began to speak through him about me, "You are not from here. God is telling me you are from a wooded area, and you haven't been able to conceive. Go home and receive your baby."

At that moment, a saw a wheel move into my feet. I didn't understand it, but I felt His presence. The wheels were turning and I heard them churn. Whoosh! Whoosh! Whoosh! I thought about Ezekiel's vision as I stood there, that awesome vision of the giant wheel within a wheel. Standing there I knew the smaller wheel I saw was different from the magnificent wheels of Ezekiel, but His presence reminded me of His Sovereign power and that it could consume me. Ezekiel saw the rims of the wheels full of eyes, searching and watching. I knew God's providence had taken over me, and I could trust the words given to me, the words spoken through the evangelist.

Before I suspected anything, I was five months along and made an appointment for a checkup. I didn't even realize my body changes because my pregnancy progressed with ease. At age thirty-six, I gave birth to Sarah, who weighed six pounds, six ounces. Because of my insurance I went back to my original doctor, who knew of my genetic condition. I brought Sarah and he said, "Oh, congratulations, you adopted again!" I said, "No, I delivered this baby myself."

God heard our prayers and, at the right time, He gave us Sarah—a miracle.

Discerning the Seasons

In my early 70s, I felt ill for a long season. I couldn't eat and my stomach burned incessantly. Insomnia left me exhausted in the day. My body shook inside, and it became so debilitating I quit traveling. Because of my passion for Muslim countries, I grieved at being unable to go. For the first time in ministry, I struggled to even be around people. When church family or friends talked to me, I'd shake. I knew something was very wrong. Depression settled in, and I thought I was dying. My doctor spent time praying with me and ran some tests. "I think I know what is wrong with you. I think you have parasites." Yet my tests didn't show this. He treated me with antibiotics, and at the end of ten days I felt better. In addition, he also advised me to seek some Christian counseling, because he suspected that there remained another healing for me. I invited two counselors to my home and mentioned the insomnia. Both discerned that it had to do with something in my past. They asked me to pray and listen for the Holy Spirit to show me. Though I had forgotten about it, when I was eleven years old, my uncle had molested me. He had repented and I forgave him a long time ago, so I knew that wasn't quite it. Then I remembered that during that dark time I had wanted to commit suicide, a typical response for a victim of sexual abuse. I believed it must have happened because something was wrong with me. The Lord spoke right then into my past, "You thought I had deserted you, but I was there all the time." He reminded me of all He did during that time, allowing me to be valedictorian of my class two years in a row and guiding me in my studies. Lovingly, He showed me the victories despite the darkness. His presence overwhelmed me, then He set me free. I cried joyful tears for three days.

Before the healing came, I felt tormented, and the enemy tried to convince me, *You will never travel again.* Then I had a dream. I was in a city in Europe somewhere, walking up a hill, the sun beaming down on me. I realized, "Hey, I'm happy. I'm walking." When I woke up, I knew the Lord wanted me to start traveling, so I phoned into the office to let them know they could start booking my calendar.

An opportunity came up to have a healing meeting in Naples, Italy, about two years later. I couldn't believe it, but when I got there I found myself on a street that felt familiar to me. Then I remembered the dream—the street where I felt the sun on me.

Healer is one of the names of God. And in our Western world of excess and technology, we have forgotten the benefits of prayer. Without prayer, we lose communication with God. I wouldn't have known consciously about the wound I still carried around from my abuse as a child, and it impacted my overall health. Through prayer, the rest of my healing came.

Throughout my years of ministry, I can say that most people, no matter where they live or what they believe about God, readily receive prayers for healing. Even atheists I've met don't refuse it. When I ask a Muslim brother or sister, "Can I pray for you?" they welcome my prayers, even in Jesus' name. In the Qu'ran, Jesus is known as a healing prophet, in fact, the only mentioned prophet who heals. So it isn't a stretch for Muslims to believe that Jesus indeed heals. We are blessed here in America with cutting edge medical care, and most everyone is able to see a doctor when illness strikes. This is a blessing, but it can also keep us from praying for God's help. I'm not at all saying to forego medical aid when you need it; rather, I'm saying because we are so blessed, we often don't pray for a miracle because of all the provisions we have that lead to healing. But in most Muslim countries, medical help is not readily available. The battles presented by poverty hold them closer to prayer as the solution. In order to go to a doctor, you have to have upfront money, so the sick often suffer through illness. The people are hungry for God's healing power.

I believe God is faithful to reveal what we can do to love our neighbor as we make ourselves available for Him to lead.

Dearborn Mosque, 2009

I smiled when I saw the announcement forwarded to me weeks before the event:

> **Tonight at IHW! Saturday, June 6, 2009 at 7:30pm**
> **Interfaith Prayer Service . . .**
>
> **For Healing, Hope, Peace & Justice—For Humanity**
>
> **Featuring . . .**
> **Imam Elahi &**
> **International Guest**
> **Dr. Marilyn Hickey**
>
> **who will share her prayer and her experience**
> **of last week's visit to Gaza.**
>
> **Followed by a reception where the communities of faith**
> **have an opportunity to come together for reflection and**
> **bridge building!**

Several years ago, while speaking at a church in Detroit, I mentioned my love for Muslims. Someone said to me, "We have 250,000 Muslims in Dearborn." I had no idea that such a high population lived just miles from where I was teaching that night. I came home and thought about it and did some praying. I'd had many healing services for Christians, but this desire to build bridges of healing kept taking over in me. I called the imam here in Denver, but I didn't get any returned calls. I talked to people about my desire to have a healing meeting for Muslims right in the United States, and the feedback didn't vary too much from, "Impossible. That is not going to happen." But I felt the urgency to try.

My friend Kimberly, who had attended my meeting in Detroit, called and said, "Marilyn, I know this Shi'ite imam from Iran." She proceeded to share with me the background of Imam Elahi. "He is the founder of the House of Wisdom, and he might be a way you can reach out to Muslims."

I pursued this potential opportunity, and Imam Elahi agreed to meet. I headed to Dearborn, where I discovered this Muslim Mecca right here in the United States.

"Mr. Elahi, I would like to have a healing meeting in a mosque." I knew God had to be the one to open this door because there had not been a healing meeting in a mosque for fourteen hundred years, and to feature a woman at such a meeting was just another obstacle. When I shared with him my heart for Muslims and my travels to more than fifty Muslim countries, a fresh breeze swept into our conversation.

"You went where? I don't know why they didn't kill you," he remarked. I told him I had been to Pakistan, one of the most dangerous countries to visit.

"I've been in Michigan now for seventeen years, and my desire is to continue to dialogue with Christians, the Jewish community, and Muslims. Let me see if this might work here in Dearborn."

He kept his word and took my request to his board. They first determined it just couldn't be done, yet we continued to dialogue. "Marilyn, next time you are in Detroit, will you come to my house for dinner?" From there the communication continued to increase, and months later we found ourselves around his dinner table. Through his hospitality, we were able to dialogue openly, and we discussed what this event might look like if I came.

"Marilyn, if you come to do this, could you pray for healing but not in the name of Jesus?"

"No, I have to. I believe Jesus is the only one who can heal. The Qu'ran even says Jesus healed the lame."

"Yes, that is very true. The ancient text says this about Jesus: 'I have come as a sign from the Lord. I heal the blind and the lepers and bring the dead to life. I inform you of what you should eat and what you should store in your houses. I was never in your house, but I know what is there,'" he confessed.

I began to share more about Jesus' healing ministry found in the four Gospels, Matthew, Mark, Luke, and John. We talked about the seventy different references in the Qu'ran to Jesus the Healing prophet, as well as the thirty-four references to Mary, His mother. Mary is the only woman mentioned in the Qu'ran. Imam Elahi allowed women to be involved in the influence of Dearborn and in leadership as well. I know the timing was right, too, because younger generations were in Dearborn, and an openness that might not have been there from previous generations allowed for us to discuss this as friends.

Before leaving, I had the opportunity to pray for his family and his wife, Jennifer. There's not a greater honor for me. Their hearts remained warm toward this fledgling friendship, and I told them, "I am your friend forever."

The event happened, and I spoke on the healing power of Jesus Christ. Though the event wasn't well attended, God used it powerfully. A boy came forward to read from the Qu'ran, and he was unable to read the banner on the back wall of the mosque. After I prayed for healing, the boy testified that his eyes had been healed. "Before you prayed, I couldn't see it, but now I can." Gratitude filled his eyes and I knew Jesus' healing power had touched this young man.

I stayed in Dearborn another night to attend a dinner with seven other imams at the House of Wisdom. Some were upset about the healing service. One imam sneered, "You should not have thrown a scene." He was letting me know I offended him—

probably on various levels. One, I was a woman preaching, and two, I am exuberant when I share about Jesus' healing and what He can do.

Though I wasn't well received by all, I know God made all of this happen. I know Imam Elahi continues to invest in our friendship. We respect each other and we agree that the world has far too much hate. The Islamic House of Wisdom is a mosque where rabbis, Christian leaders, and imams can sit around a table all at once. We don't have to agree on our beliefs about God to establish a friendship.

Imam Elahi told me that some of the attendees experienced God's presence during the healing meeting. He shared, "We consider your prayers for us a source of hope and energy. When prayers come from a sincere soul, it makes all the difference." As we continue to grow a friendship, I know, the Lord will lead me in what that looks like.

6

muslims within reach

Follow the way of love. . . .

—1 Corinthians 14:1

Relationships show the fruit of our lives and often reveal what we are called to do. Usually our calling starts with the community around us, or at least involves the community around us. Some opportunities are right under our noses, and I have found that to be true over and over again.

Several years ago, I needed a transportation service to accommodate my frequent trips to the airport. I stumbled upon an Iranian Muslim family with a dependable business. Some might take issue with the fact that I didn't seek out a Christian company, but God really laid it on my heart to use their car and shuttling service. I first became acquainted with the eldest son, David, who obviously had a strong entrepreneurial spirit. I began to ask him about his family story and how they had come to the United States. I took a personal interest in him. David showed me a great deal of respect, and as I got to know him, I invited his whole family over for Easter dinner. It gave me great joy to host them on Resurrection Sunday, for Christians the pinnacle time of worship. I felt honored when they agreed to come. From that time on, I've continued to invite them over for dinner, though it can be challenging to find a time when everyone in the family can come. Recently Tara, David's younger sister, started coming to church on a regular basis. I know that building a relationship has impacted her desire to come and to learn more about the Bible.

I can't think of a better way to spend a Friday night than having a potluck with a Muslim family along with some of my close friends. It's something I try to do whenever I can. Chicken casserole alongside Tandoori chicken makes the miles in our hearts come together faster than any other platform I know. The discussions are always lively, and the burdens of life along with the celebrations are very much the same. When we gather, I don't like anyone to leave who hasn't been prayed for, so I ask both my Christian friends and my Muslim friends a simple question, "How can I pray for you?" At a recent gathering, David's father said, "I ask that we pray for peace." And his mother's request was, "Pray for my health." And strange as it sounds, I'm able to pray for my Christian friends and my Muslim friends right in my living room together. There's an unspoken blessing when you share food, a bit of your life, and prayer together.

These dinners have sprouted many meaningful dialogues about God, and I don't ever want to pass up an opportunity to pray for their needs. To extend hospitality gives me an opportunity to show that I care and love them just for who they are, and there is something about being invited to someone's home—you feel accepted.

Through our different times gathered around the dinner table, I've been able to get to know David's parents, who came to the States to find better business opportunities and to provide more choices and freedoms for their children. And Tara, too, who is like most every twentysomething in America, searching and wanting to find love and the good life. Colorado is where she grew up, so she is accustomed to Westernized thinking and living. Tara exudes genuine warmth; she's approachable and open about her feelings and future hopes. I'll never forget the time I returned from an extended teaching tour and she and David greeted me at the airport with flowers for Mother's Day. She considers me to be another "mom" in her life, and I treasure that.

It isn't always easy to pursue a growing friendship when there are real differences in beliefs, but I try to be consistent, letting them know I'm praying for them and thinking of them by sending a text or an email here and there. Friendship grows through staying committed to reaching out, and so sometimes there are great strides forward, and sometimes you can't seem to make schedules work and differing lifestyles present issues. But God reminds me if I continue to walk with them He'll continue to lead.

Reaching Out to Dearborn

I still marvel at how God set up the Dearborn event and showed me a whole community of Muslims right outside of Detroit. My relationship with the Elahi family continues well past the miraculous doors that opened at the mosque, Islamic House of Wisdom, in 2009. I believe one of the bridges God has used to keep my relationship with the Elahis in a place of growth is our mutual trust of one another. Through my connection with the International House of Wisdom, I had the privilege of getting to know Jennifer, Imam Elahi's wife, and learned more about her story.

Planning the Dearborn event took several meetings, and a big part of the planning involved getting to know one another, just as friends. From the start, Jennifer didn't hide her emotions or her excitement that I had agreed to come. When she found out I wanted to pray for the families at the mosque, she was moved with deep gratitude. I shared about my travels over the last few decades, the events we planned in Sudan, Pakistan, and other Muslim countries, and I attested to God's healing power I had witnessed over Muslims. Imam Elahi and Jennifer both respected my outreach because they both knew my mission wasn't an easy one. When they realized I'd been to about fifty Muslim countries, it became clear to them that I wasn't doing this for any other reason than out of love for fellow humanity. We see our friendship as sincere, and though we differ on matters of faith, Imam Elahi, Jennifer, and I all desired to build bridges and move away from the pain of 9/11. And dialogue leads to understanding. Jennifer shared her heart with a great deal of honesty:

> Marilyn, it's hard to be a Muslim woman in 2012. After 9/11, Muslim women have been the target. I had an incident happen that made me realize how deep the rift runs. In the parking lot of a grocery store, a car sped up close enough to hit my arm while I was pushing my son in the cart toward the entrance doors. . . . I also remember when we headed out for a peace conference and some New York City fire fighters harassed us on the airplane, telling us to go back to our country. The airline did refund our ticket costs due to the harassment we experienced, so that helped us to realize not everyone felt we were anti-American. People assume because you dress modestly and wear a *hijab* that you are uneducated or ignorant and don't speak English.

The prejudices Jennifer encountered are real, painful conflicts within her community. I know that there aren't easy answers in discerning what relationships look like when we continue to live in a world full of hate. Jennifer desires to educate those in her community about what the Islamic House of Wisdom believes and to support other women trying to live out the tensions that exist between culture and faith. Through her work at the mosque, Jennifer's wants the community of Dearborn to know that violence is never the answer. Hate is not the answer.

Imam Elahi said to me, "Marilyn, a good friend is a great gift.

It can bring wisdom and maturity, prosperity, pleasure, and protection." Imam Elahi came to the States twenty years ago in pursuit of interfaith work. He gathers with rabbis, Christian clergy, and political leaders of his community to better their awareness of the issues of the day. "Our mosque is unique in that we desire discussion among those we differ from, but more than that we desire community cooperation. We want to support the poor, women in leadership, and work together. The biggest obstacles I have found in working with diverse leaders are selfishness, arrogance, and ignorance. . . . Hate is very dangerous, and we speak out against Islamophobia. Extremists have wrongly killed both Christians and Muslims."

Imam Elahi and Jennifer continue to show me how God can use Christians in the lives of Muslims. Both respect me for speaking directly about my faith in Jesus Christ, and our friendship is strong enough for open conversations. The fact that I never waver on the essentials of my faith makes them respect me all the more.

When the planning for the Dearborn event started, Jennifer shared openly about her own personal storm. After two months of testing, her doctor told her she needed to have a D and C surgery because of a miscarriage. As this was her first pregnancy, the fear of future fertility issues weighed down on her. Yet she wanted to be a part of our discussions and move outside of her own personal sorrow. We prayed together about her condition and she shared with me the seeds of hope that she felt growing inside of her, despite this real loss. God used our fellowship in a timely way for Jennifer.

Jennifer desires to be an advocate for women. And although Muslim men are often thought to be the ones who oppress women, Imam Elahi supports his wife's ideas and passions. She desires to start a job-training center for those in need of new marketable skills in a tough economy. The mosque also serves a local soup kitchen alongside other ministries in the community. Jennifer speaks out openly against the oppression of women and continues to look for ways to provide humanitarian relief for those in Dearborn.

I think about the tax collectors in the Bible—the most despised class of people. They cheated the taxpayers by charging them whatever they wished at their own whim. Even beggars wouldn't take money from them. If we look at the despised in our society today, Muslim groups might be the lowest of the low, the ones not worthy of receiving help because of radicals who were driven by forces of evil. For me, I believe God has asked me to take a step toward Muslims in my path, not a step away, to watch what He will do. When I'm in the Detroit area, I try to call Imam Elahi and check on how his family is doing; I always offer up a prayer for whatever burden they might be facing. The political tensions we face are real, but friendship approaches the person as an image bearer of God, drawing the worst enemy within your reach.

7

mani's story

As he neared Damascus on his journey, suddenly a light from heaven flashed around him. He fell to the ground and heard a voice say to him, "Saul, Saul, why do you persecute me?" "Who are you, Lord?" Saul asked. "I am Jesus, whom you are persecuting," he replied. "Now get up and go into the city, and you will be told what you must do."

—ACTS 9:3–6

There are times when there is no way to explain a door that opens, other than the providence of God. I marvel at the steady cadence of life that pulsates with the spin of free will cooperating with His Sovereign plan. It never unfolds as you think it will. It's always better. More mysterious. My friendship with Mani has been guided by the hand of God. But years before we met, God invaded his life in a supernatural way. Not everyone experiences such a supernatural conversion like Mani did—his darkest day of existence actually turned into his day of salvation. God often works in left field, and in 1997, Mani met His Savior when he wasn't looking for Him.

Mani grew up in Iran as a Shi'ite Muslim. But in day-to-day life, his faith didn't inform his behavior or impact the course of his life. The members of his family weren't practicing Muslims, so they did not go to mosque or worship Allah on a regular basis.

Yet there was loyalty to the name *Muslim* and identifying with it culturally, just as many Americans identify culturally with the name *Christian*.

His family moved to Florida, and Mani began to attend university. He encountered many Christians when he came to the United States, and he found himself getting into arguments when he talked to them, even though he held no conviction to Islamic teachings.

Often God has more opportunity to work in our lives when we encounter loss, when we have to look for answers beyond ourselves or beyond hopeless circumstances. When Mani was a junior in college, the tragedies in his life began to overtake him. Felony charges rose up against him, though he was innocent. His wife left him, leaving him alone to face his accusers, and his penalties included losing his student status at the university. Mani lost all his drive for success and direction. In a flash, all that Mani considered to be of value disappeared. But during his time at the University of Florida, he had met two men, Jeff and Tom, who showed a sincere interest in him. Before the tragic chain of events, Mani found himself in the middle of a genuine friendship, so much so he entrusted the two students with the despair he felt, and they reached out with empathy, not judgment, and prayed for Mani. The possible twenty-year jail sentence he faced led Mani to suicidal thoughts. Jeff and Tom continued to share the hope of their faith in what God could do to help, but Mani didn't grasp what they were telling him about Jesus. And yet they continued to reach out in love. Depression and anxiety began to torment Mani. Sleepless nights and haunting hopelessness set in, and being alone fed into his misery. Waiting on a court date, enduring the nightmare for another four months, took Mani's thoughts toward more darkness. No family support and no wife— just these two Christian friends. But he found himself continually leaning on them, trusting them.

"Mani, we'd like to invite you to a business retreat. Will you come?"

Mani had $180 to his name and the cost of the conference was $150.

"Yes. I will go." Mani didn't go because of an interest in the conference; rather he trusted his friends and it gave him an opportunity to be around them and not be alone. On the third night, Jeff and Tom asked him to attend an evening function in the hotel, which happened to be a church service. Not wanting to be rude, Mani came and heard the sermon . . . but didn't listen. At the end, the pastor invited anyone in the audience to come forward for prayer and to accept Jesus Christ as Lord and Savior. Mani stood with the others who gathered around each round table, though not engaged with the words he heard from the platform. But then God took over:

"I stood up and someone came and pushed me forward, and I looked back with agitation, but didn't see anyone. I figured at that point it was my imagination, so I stood back up again as the altar call continued and then I felt the push again from behind. Again, I didn't see anyone. My heart started to race and I felt panicked. The third time the speaker asked for people to come forward, my knees buckled and I fell. By the fourth and fifth time he said, "There is one person who needs to come. . . . We are waiting." Mani resisted, but he felt multiple forces holding him back.

Still collapsed on his knees, Mani couldn't move. He then felt the pressure of relief as he walked toward the front, but he feared what was happening to him. After the service, Jeff asked, "How did you like the service?" Out of courtesy Mani told him it was fine. But then he couldn't stop the words from forming on his lips, "I accepted the Lord Jesus Christ as Lord and Savior." Bewildered, he stood there looking at Jeff, not comprehending what he had said.

Tom shouted, "Wow, that is amazing!" Mani then grabbed his bags and ran out of the banquet room. Another conference attendee stopped him as he ran through the hall and said, "How are you doing?" Again, he confessed Jesus as Lord and turned around running again. But he ended up running straight toward the preacher. Involuntarily, Mani confessed Jesus as Lord a third time.

As he reached his hotel room, he fell to his knees and prayed to God, "I don't know what I've just done or said. I don't understand it. I'm certainly in trouble. I need a miracle and I need help. I . . . I don't know . . . help me. I cannot go to jail for something I have not done. If you don't help me, I will kill myself. God, please save me. If you do, then I will serve you for the rest of my life. And I'm praying in the name of Jesus, as these people proclaim here tonight."

Immediately the weight fell off of his body. The bondage of his burdens turned to joy and he started singing. He packed up his things and drove home. For the first time in months, he slept. And then the miracles followed. The next day he went to the bank knowing that he only had $20 left, but the balance on his account read $2000. He knew it had to be a mistake, so he spoke to the banker and told her that a deposit had wrongly been applied to his account. She claimed it was Mani's. He had prayed for a miracle, and this indeed came from a heavenly source.

Mani hadn't heard from his lawyer in some time; he didn't even know if he remembered his case or not. The phone rang. He couldn't believe what he was hearing over the phone, "Mani, I have good news. I talked to the judge and I have been following your case, and I realized that this has been done improperly. I know you are innocent, and we can prove this." Another miracle had taken place. Mani couldn't deny that God had heard his prayers.

With the charges dropped, Mani re-enrolled in school and

had another supernatural encounter. His ex-wife was standing in the street near the campus, waiting for a ride. She spotted Mani's care and came over.

"The charges have been dropped. There is now proof of my innocence!" From there, the reconciliation process began for Mani and his wife. In a matter of days, God turned Mani's life around, giving him back all that had been lost.

Mani remembered what he told God; he knew he had to keep his end of the bargain. He called the only two people he knew who had been there for him and told them everything that happened. "Can you get me a Bible and help me go to church so I can be a good Christian?" These faithful friends came again to offer support and took him to a Bible-believing church. That Sunday the pastor preached on salvation. And though he had heard the words of the preacher at the conference, it all sounded new to him. Mani confessed, "Once I grasped the gift, I was overjoyed, and I asked my friends, 'Why didn't you ever tell me about salvation?'" Well, they had, but he didn't perceive it. And then they confessed, "Mani, we've been praying for you ever since we met."

Mani knew he couldn't turn his back on God now, not after these days of miracles. He knew what had gotten him to the business conference—his friends had been praying for his salvation. They knew God had a plan for his life. Mani claimed to be an agnostic Muslim at best, so his religious ties were not strong. All of Mani's foundational questions about God were answered in the months that followed his radical conversion.

About two years later, Mani had a revelation about his conversion experience. God told him he had had a "Peter experience." The Lord led him to the story of Peter, who denied Jesus three times. Peter didn't want to deny Jesus, but he did. The Holy Spirit reminded Mani how he didn't want to confess His Name, but it came out of his mouth. Peter denied Jesus three times, though he did not want to, so it was a Peter experience, but in reverse. His immediate family soon learned about his conversion, and they weren't happy about it, but he didn't at all feel persecuted for embracing Christianity.

God is the true Seeker, and Mani's two friends faithfully built a bridge. And because of that bridge, I met Mani several years later at his local church. Mani heard me say very openly from the platform, "I love Muslims and my heart is to reach out to them. I believe God will allow me to go to Iran and have a healing meeting."

The pastor of the church arranged for me to meet Mani after the service. Mani then told me about his work with Iranian satellite TV programming.

"Marilyn, can you come to the station and share your teachings with Iranians? I'm amazed at your willingness to go to Muslim countries despite the difficult hurdles. Not many evangelists want to go." After our meeting, we made plans about how I might encourage Muslims, and by the end of 2009 I made my way to San Jose, California, where I went on, live, to the audience in Iran. People started calling in at our station; they were so excited to hear our programs. I knew this blessing God orchestrated and to know that the underground church leaders in Iran benefited from this satellite TV fueled my spirit all the more. Six to seven hundred thousand people now accessed Christian programming. Though the government discourages such programming, it's difficult to stop it. People can watch it from Internet cafes, and it is increasingly hard to block; sometimes the government can confiscate a satellite, but often it is just sold again to make money.

Young people and women are resisting government oppression, and they want to be able to make their own choices. Mani reminds me that he cannot go and be a bridge because they see him as a convert, therefore marked. So I want to go and trust God to build relationships.

Mani's Ministry

God is the best networker of all. Years before we met, God set Mani up to do great things to share the love of Christ. After several years of studying Scripture, seeking God for direction, Mani knew his calling involved ministering to Iranian people. In 2001, he found himself pastoring a church of about one hundred, a congregation made up of Muslim converts. Most of them were Iranians who were curious and had been impacted by someone who became saved. Many came because of the fellowship and the love they encountered.

During this time, the Lord impressed upon Mani that he would be sharing the Gospel with Iranians on TV, though he had no idea how. After 9/11, it seemed more impossible than ever before for Christian programming to be available in Iran. He began to create programs in Farsi and, in faith, put them on the shelf for future use, waiting for that open door.

A friend who had connections in television told Mani of a need for Iranian TV and felt convinced that God wanted to use Mani, that Iran was being neglected. Despite the terror of September 11, Mani signed a contract in December 2001 for $500 a month to create the first Christian broadcasting in Iran. The reach spread to 2 million viewers on a weekly basis.

When Mani asked me to share some of my teachings, I jumped at the chance. Again, the open door presented itself, and I knew God had worked it out in advance. Mani's heart for the Middle East is contagious, and revival is happening there. Between 1857 and 1978, in a nation of seven million, the number of known Muslim conversions to Christianity numbered around twelve hundred souls, though illegal under the Shah. Currently, Mani reports that there are around one million. The growth has been fueled by TV programming.

Through Mani's connection with Iranian TV, the underground church in Iran receives encouragement through severe persecution. A few years ago, he asked me to go along, to teach specifically on Jesus' healing ministry. We met in a private location and the people's gratitude toward me is something that remains so precious to me. Because all of the Christians are willing to die for their faith, their love for God is so obvious. Mani shared with me how few leaders are willing to come in to encourage these faithful believers. There isn't the pomp and circumstance that surrounds crusade meetings; perhaps some Christian leaders decline because the crowd is small. My previous work with the underground church in China fueled my desire to go and be a blessing to leaders in need of encouragement. With about a hundred of us gathered for a few days, I found that *they* actually encouraged *me*. They didn't tire of hearing the lessons and wanted to go on into the wee hours of the night, never tiring of hearing God's Word.

In Iran, the persecution for believers within Mani's network is not as frequent as in some other circles; they do all they can to protect them. However, there are traps to catch coverts. Some Christians are serving time in jail, waiting for their release. A recent case of persecution happened in a city where a Christian woman of the underground church ministered to a married Muslin woman and she converted. The husband found out and retaliated with a trap, pretending that he, too, wanted to convert. Elated with her husband's words, she told a few Christian leaders, who then broke protocol and went directly to the husband. Upon arriving, those serving this family found the militia waiting to arrest them.

One of the faithful believers, Brother Omar, endured harsh conditions when thrown into his cell for assisting Christians. The guards hung him upside down and he survived extreme cold conditions. Several times they soaked him in water, and the harsh treatment on his body took its toll. Pneumonia set in, but this godly man prayed in faith in his prison cell. Miraculously, God healed him. He remembers having a cough, asking God to keep him warm in the drafty cell. "Lord, heat the ground of this prison cell." And the floor grew warm. God's grace surrounded him, through fifteen days of torture. Upon release, Omar waited for his date before the courts to receive his long-term jail sentence. Often a prisoner is sent to another city after sixty days. Two months passed by, and the courts eventually forgot about the case and dropped his sentence. By inaction of the court, those involved were set free, never having to go back to see the judge. These faithful believers, willing to endure more persecution, moved and started a ministry elsewhere. It's not uncommon for those working with the underground church to end up in jail for six months to a year, with no communication with any circle of support. These leaders rely on prayer and faith.

When Mani learned about the vision I had from God to preach in Iran, he didn't seem surprised at all. He didn't think it strange that God chose to call a red-headed, eighty-year-old woman to the Middle East. He believes I'm to go there soon and believes God will open the right doors. I don't have any idea when, but I do know the passion rises up in me to share with those who have not heard how much God loves them. Everyone deserves to hear about the healing power of Jesus Christ, and we both agree there is a divine purpose in our relationship. And that is the wild thing about God. Did I ever set out to go into nations that don't allow religious freedom? No. But I believe that with God, all things are possible, even in the most oppressed nations of this world. No one thought the wall of communism would fall down, but the world witnessed it. With God, a nation can change in a day.

8

the price tag of being a good samaritan

*I am only one, but I am one. I cannot do everything, but I
can do something. And I will not let what I cannot do
interfere with what I can do.*

—EDWARD EVERETT HALE

Ray began his morning routine and sat down to breakfast. As he
sat down by the kitchen window, he spotted a child floating down
the drainage ditch outside. Immediately, he rushed out of his
house and jumped in the water. Ray knew the water flowed to the
culvert ahead at the bridge. He grabbed hold of a rock and determined, *I'm not going to let go, and I'm going to hold on, hold on
with all my might.* From there, he swept up the little girl out of the
grip of the water. Emergency vehicles arrived and saw how Ray
managed to pull this eight-year-old child out and save her. They
were amazed he had the strength to do this. The city officials
honored their hero, but here is what really makes him heroic:
Ray didn't know how to swim. His compassion and hope took
over and compelled him to jump in, no matter if it meant losing
his life. He display of love for his fellow neighbor inspired his
entire community.

My neighbor, Sue, is puzzled over my passion for Muslims.
Sue understands and supports what I do to teach the Bible at my
church and within Christian circles, but she doesn't understand

why I love Muslims. "Marilyn, you are just going to get yourself killed over there. Shouldn't you just stay here where it is safer for you?" I responded with an honest question, "Are you going to go? . . . Well, that is why I'm going. Someone has to go."

Jesus tells a compelling parable of the Good Samaritan that puts the word *neighbor* into perspective. In Luke 10, Jesus is talking with the religious leaders. On many occasions, they tested Jesus and wanted to trap Him into answering within their narrow perspective. And they added regulations to the Law that were not there, like healing on the Sabbath, which Jesus did joyfully. This religious leader steps up and says, "What must I do to inherit eternal life?" Jesus throws the question back on the man with another question: "How do you read it? What does the Law really say?" He quotes, "Love the Lord your God with all your heart, with all your strength, soul, and mind, and love your neighbor as yourself." Jesus tells the man he answered correctly. But then the religious leader poses the question, "But who is my neighbor?" And then Jesus sets him up with the truth.

The man wanted to justify himself, but Jesus' wisdom points him down a road that exposes his motives. This religious leader wanted to confine his neighbor to his own comfortable borders. Jesus uses a Samaritan to be the hero, the least likely. Samaritans were despised by the Jews. Think of the most difficult people to love in your proximity. Would it be the homeless, the prostitutes, or a Muslim even?

Good Samaritan is a term we use today to mean a benevolent person. We don't see it as a hostile term or think of a Samaritan as an outcast. But Jesus carefully sets up the parable in such a way that the leaders must rethink about how a willingness to love others reflects how much they understand God's love for them.

A man was going down the road from to Jerusalem to Jericho and was stopped by abusive and violent robbers. The Greek word used for robber means "villain," someone who is just hurting someone for the pleasure of it. This Jewish man was stripped, robbed, and beaten—left for dead. These robbers beat the life out of him, and his chances of survival were fifty-fifty.

A priest walked by, saw the halfway dead man lying in the road, and crossed over to the other side of the road. How many of us have done that when we see a panhandler? And if we are honest, how many of us avoid a "neighbor" because of our prejudices? It's just easier to pretend someone doesn't exist. It's easy to be intimidated by the black *hijab* a Muslim woman wears over her head as she passes by on the same street as you and me, to ignore the fact she is a neighbor. *Neighbor* means "those who are close." The priest tried to *not* be close and kept walking. And then Jesus said the group of Levites passed right by as well. The Levites, too, were most likely traveling back from worship at the temple in Jerusalem and also considered to be holy men in close circles with the priests of the day. They had *just* finished proclaiming their love for God—and yet walked by their neighbor.

Their attitude matched the priest's. Jesus exposed the religiosity of people in this story—those we'd naturally think might have saved the man first had a faith that didn't impact their actions. A dead man was considered unclean, so perhaps the excuse for a Levite might have been, "Well, I don't want to be unclean for worship," but the reality is they were journeying home. They already worshipped God. Jesus exposed the Levites' lifeless faith.

There are so many reasons we can neglect our neighbor— too busy, too scared, too tired, too stressed. All of that may be true, but Jesus points to sacrificial love over and over again. A recent case study conducted at a seminary revealed the same behavioral struggles found in the priest and Levites. Twenty students completed a study on the Parable of the Good Samaritan and then prepared a presentation as part of a class project.

Those conducting the experiment did not tell the students the objective but that they would be called to present at different times. Each student encountered a person who appeared to have been beaten up on the way to the presentation. Eighty percent of the students passed by the victim—on their way to illustrate a presentation on the Good Samaritan. How easy it is to step over someone when we are in a hurry, set on a task. But God wants us to see everyone in our path. This is how He instructs us to live and what illustrates our love for God—loving our neighbor. What the religious leader wanted to know from Jesus was, "How far out toward the fringes of humanity do I have to love?" He wanted an out through a technicality.

It's easy to justify why we do not extend a benevolent hand: "Oh, the guy deserved it. He shouldn't be traveling on the road at night." Or, "If I help that guy, he will abuse my help. He just needs to get a job." A pastor and his leadership in New York set out to help a struggling single mom with four kids. She lived right next to the church. The pastor approached her and found out she had a lot of debt. Graciously, he told her "Some of our deacons will gather some money and help you with your debt." So they brought enough money to pay her bills and relieve some of her burdens. But the mother then went out and bought brand new bikes and expensive clothes and took the kids out to a nice restaurant. Then she didn't have enough to pay her bills. Along the way, the church leadership found out how she spent the money. Some complained, "Our help was wasted. We aren't going to help her anymore."

As the pastor talked with her, he realized the truth from her perspective. She said, "I feel responsible to be both father and mother. My kids don't have nice clothes and the food they eat is mainly to survive. They always feel like they never belong. For once, I wanted them to feel like everybody else. That's why I did it."

From there, the church decided to get involved in the mother's life. They helped the kids in school and provided tutors. They helped the mother with money management. The deacons began to actually see the world through the eyes of an exhausted mom and entered into the real struggle with her. When we have the mentality that a certain type of neighbor is unworthy of help, then we won't rise up as a hero of hope. But Jesus asks us to be on the side of anyone created in His image because *He* is. Everyone bears the image of God. Historically, America has been a blessed nation, and we love siding with the winning team. But the truth is that God is for the victim, the poor, even the people who make bad decisions. We, ourselves, want the generosity of God, but we withhold it from others.

Jesus strategically uses the Samaritan man as the hero of the story, the one considered worse than a tax collector or worse than a Gentile—outside the realm of having any worth in society. In this probing story, Jesus served humble pie to his audience of religious leaders, who claimed to be the spiritually elite, the true worshippers. Luke 10:33 says that the despised Samaritan felt deep compassion for the wounded man. The Greek word for compassion doesn't mean an expression of pity, but rather it's an intense, deep feeling that comes from the core of a person. For a Samaritan to walk over toward the Jewish victim was an impossible idea to a Jew because they knew Samaritans were victims—spat on, ridiculed, and mocked by Jews. He bandages his wounds with the traveling medicine kit of the day—oil and wine—and then hoists him up on his donkey and takes him to an inn, gives the innkeeper two denarii, and even says, "If you need more I'll be back to reconcile the bill."

Then Jesus asks the religious leaders, "Who proved to be the neighbor in the story?" The man who questions Jesus just couldn't bring himself to say the word *Samaritan* so he says, "the one who showed mercy." Love doesn't ask, "How far out of my way do I need to go?" But rather love asks, "What can I do to help?" When we put conditions on our lives, the lines of our prejudices become glaringly obvious.

Rescuing Ruth and Sarah, Saving Moses

As a proud mother, I watched my daughter, Sarah, wrestle with *Who is my neighbor?* in an extraordinary way. God seized Sarah's heart when she came back from a mission trip in Ethiopia. And at just the right time, a friend of hers challenged her with some timely questions: "What is God calling you to do? What are some of the different ways God wants to use your life?" I've loved seeing Sarah's love for biblical languages unfold—we have that in common—but God's plan usually unfolds in layers, and I see that for Sarah. She recognized God's steady tug, pushing her to more of what He had for her to do. Through ministry travels to orphanages and medical clinics in impoverished countries in Africa and Asia, Sarah met her unexpected neighbors, the smallest ones, who are the most unattended populace in the world, ages zero to five. The blueprint of how she was to love a neighbor started to surface.

After having three children of her own, Sarah saw the struggling mothers in Ethiopia, Angola, and Cambodia in a very personal way. Mothers fear childbirth because most are faced with either no medical aid at all or unsanitary medical clinics. But then if a mother and newborn survive labor, the responsibility to provide daily nourishment and medical needs means to live well beyond their abilities.

During a trip to a Jewish village in Ethiopia, Sarah met twin babies, Ruth and Sarah. In talking with those who ran the village orphanage, she learned that it wasn't common practice to take infants due to the medical expenses and the needed around-the-clock care. The police contacted the orphanage after finding the babies in an open field. As Sarah held them, her motherly instincts overwhelmed her as she wondered how long the twins had been alone. Who saw them and just walked on by? Were they crying? Why? After placing them back in the crib, she ran outside to gasp for air, to thank God these precious twin girls had a safe place, but then also to deal with her anger as she thought of infants and helpless children who were not safe.

Upon Sarah's return home, the experience grew in her heart as she prayed, trying to answer her friend's challenge, "What does God want you to do with your life?" She continued to remember the twins, Sarah and Ruth. She remembered their frail bodies but also the strength in their eyes. Her passion to save babies welled up inside her, though she had no idea how to go about it. And time to give to such an effort seemed impossible for Sarah, who was juggling family life, ministry needs, and her studies in biblical languages. Yet she couldn't put off what she knew, that the single biggest cause of infant mortality was malnutrition and lives could be saved.

Most of the time when we commit to help a neighbor, some kind of risk is involved, some kind of cost. Sarah found a way in the busiest time of her life, eliminating pursuits like her doctoral studies and honing in to focus on these vulnerable neighbors she met. And there, somewhere between prayer, assessing goals, and listening to God, *Saving Moses* started.

Sarah's research continues as she seeks to help provide nutrition, medical care, and even education for mothers in need in impoverished countries. In Cambodia, which has the third highest infant mortality rate in Asia, mothers resort to prostitution so that they can feed their babies—a real and harsh struggle. Babies are often chained under the bed when a client comes to the room and the mother sells herself to save her child. *Saving Moses* is working to set up night care facilities for babies who have nowhere to go but under a bed while a mother is forced to sell herself. The needs of the vulnerable are undeniable, and when we take time to gaze upon a hurting neighbor, to see the dignity in their struggle, we can be a part of their road to redemption. Sarah and her team have witnessed how hope can grow from an undefined passion, growing in a heart, toward a neighbor . . . even a neighbor halfway around the world who is a victim.

The Samaritan man knew what it felt like to be a victim. Perhaps that is why he had compassion for the Jewish man who lay half dead. Jesus wants us to grapple with the question: "Is my love for my neighbor exclusive or inclusive?" If we sow exclusivity then we will be exclusive, limiting what God can do through us.

I think back to when God saved me from my sin and I accepted Him as my Savior at age sixteen—the freedom I felt and how I wanted to spend the rest of my life sharing that freedom. Everyone deserves to hear about Jesus and His healing power. It's not for me to be concerned if they reject it. And in so many places, the Bible indicates I shouldn't be the one to judge who is worthy or unworthy of my help. I just know I'm called to go and help my neighbor, whether it's a Muslim on my street or a Muslim in Pakistan. I want to be like the Good Samaritan. I want to walk with my neighbor, even if it means there is great risk involved.

As any human being wrestles with the question, "Who is my neighbor?" it comes down to us answering, "What kind of life do I want to live? Do we want to live a sedentary life or a transformational life?" A sedentary neighbor might say, "Oh, I feel so sorry for the homeless," as he drives by in a warm car with a hot cup of coffee in the drink holder. To notice the needs of others is at least a start, but I don't believe it is where God wants us to stay. The Good Samaritan became part of the solution. We have a choice. We can live sacrificially or selfishly. The Good Samaritan holds us to a high standard. He provided physical protection, medical aid, and shelter to an enemy. The enemy often is our neighbor.

Out on the Fringes

When we reach out toward the fringes of a community, toward those the world somehow has made unworthy of help, there will be criticism. Many Christians I respect do not feel called to reach out to Muslims at all, and sometimes I'm not understood. I don't discount the well-meaning warnings of friends and family who are concerned about the dangers involved in traveling to countries still raging in civil wars and trying to live in peace. I do understand that 9/11 happened, that this war between Christianity and Islam has been going on for centuries, and that there are real risks and a cost to count.

I'm not certain why God has given me such favor with Muslims and Muslim countries, but God is a God who opens doors when we ask for help. I made a promise to God that I would do as He commanded, "Love your neighbor as yourself." I know I'm to walk in His favor and see all that God can do. I trust Him to lead me now while I'm in my eighties, more than I've ever trusted Him to lead me when I was in my thirties. I've prayed for a long life, so that I can go and find a Muslim neighbor in need of hope and healing. And I do believe He will lead me to every neighbor He wants me to help.

9

favor in pakistan

You prepare a table before me in the presence of my enemies;
You anoint my head with oil;
My cup runs over.
Surely goodness and mercy shall follow me
All the days of my life;
And I will dwell in the house of the Lord
Forever.

—Psalm 23:5–6 nkjv

Before departing from DIA, we gathered for prayer. The scripture read was Exodus 33:14: "The Lord replied, 'I will personally go with you, Moses, and I will give you rest—everything will be fine for you.'" Stephen had flown out five days ahead of us to make sure we were in good standing with Karachi officials. After years and months of planning, maneuvering through impossible doors in a post–bin Laden country, and postponing dates, we were certain now was the time for our event.

You're coming home in a box. This is it for you, Marilyn. The enemy badgered me with thoughts of discouragement as I sat in my seat, trying to focus on praying. Thankfully, I recognized where those thoughts were coming from and continued to believe the timing and days ahead were all planned as the work God had for our hands in January of 2012. I'd been there six times, and for whatever reason, God continually had targeted Pakistan as a place of ministry. I'm not sure why I've had such favor, particularly in this Muslim country, but I know, too, that I can't get hung up on *why* so much—I must just trust Him.

I really couldn't believe it. We were here. By the grace of God, we made it back to Pakistan, seven years later. I'm always a bit uncomfortable with the way they fuss over us when we arrive. Rose petals lined the tarmac when we stepped out of the aircraft, and then they ballyhooed me around in a horse-drawn carriage with four white horses. "Hallelujah!" shouted out the welcoming citizens of Karachi. Bagpipes and drums accompanied our welcome parade, ending with the release of a multi-colored bouquet of balloons. Any time I've been to Pakistan, the pageantry of the welcoming committee has always outdone the visit before, making you feel quite unworthy of it all.

As I settled into the hotel room in Karachi, I picked up the current issue of *Time* magazine, which contained a story titled "Pakistan's Dark Heart." This only reinforced our favor to be an act of God. Looking back, I marvel at all God did to assure us that He personally was with us. An article specifically on Karachi called it "the world's most dangerous city," a land that had hosted more than a thousand people in ethnic turf wars over the last year, fueled by the main political parties. Its streets were polluted with hand grenades and explosives. British author, academic, and terrorism analyst Anatol Lieven called Pakistan "perhaps the biggest and wobbliest domino on the world stage." The recent surge in violence had sealed Karachi's reputation as being unlivable, a hub of political aggression. But then take away the political wars and you still have armed robbery, kidnapping for ransom, and murder—policed with only thirty thousand underpaid men in a city with a population of approximately 18 million.

And yet I had felt an overwhelming sense of God's peace right when we landed, unaware of the threatening headlines.

Tremendous peace. The oppressive thoughts had disappeared long before arriving. Knowing of all the turmoil, our team committed to pray for one thing—peace over this country. To be in a Muslim city that is known as the most dangerous in the world and yet experience the peace of God right in the midst of conflict, was greater confirmation that He had orchestrated all of this for us. This healing meeting had been bathed in prayer, with thousands of intercessors in Pakistan and so many back home in the States. It was like seeing heaven come down upon us in a very up close kind of way, like Jesus told us to pray—in an *on earth as it is in heaven* kind of way.

January 17, 2012, marked our first event, an evening reception given for 160 dignitaries from Karachi and Islamabad. Guests included pastors from around Pakistan, imams, priests, and political representatives. The dignitaries who spoke encouraged unity through differences. Moulana, an imam; Mrs. Baji Jaleel, a senior official with Muttahida Quami Movement (MQM); and political figure Rauf Siddiqui, the minister of industries and commerce, all spoke of a heartfelt desire for peace.

As I looked around the banquet hall, I recognized some leaders I had met years ago. Some graciously came up to me and said, "You prayed for me years ago, and Jesus healed me." I was also aware of martyred Christian leaders who were not present. I celebrated their faith, too, as they paved the way to continue opening doors for us. A young boy came to my table and placed a beautiful bouquet of orchids in front of me. "Dr. Hickey, thank you for praying for Mother and Father," he said with a proud heart. "My father is Abraham, your interpreter for Lahore 2003. You prayed for them to have children. We thank you for praying. I am here now!" When you get to see the fruit of prayer standing in front of you, you realize God's overwhelming faithfulness.

As I looked around at the tables of dignitaries and their families, I wanted more than ever to communicate Jesus' desire to heal people in Pakistan. I felt an urgency to not mess around. In the past, we had to build trust and tread lightly at times, but a boldness rose up in me to pray for healing in this first gathering.

"Do you know why I came to Karachi? It's because Jesus wants to heal Pakistani people. I've witnessed His healing power reach down to the people of Sudan, Morocco, and Lahore. Jesus wants to heal you, too.

"How many of you have a broken heart?" Twenty stood. I felt led to pray for those with ailing feet and bad ankles and knees. About fifteen stood. Religious leader Maulana Shah Rehmani stood and testified that his knee pain left him.

God laid Psalm 2 on my heart:

Why do the nations conspire
    and the peoples plot in vain?
The kings of the earth rise up
    and the rulers band together
    against the Lord and against his anointed, saying,
"Let us break their chains
    and throw off their shackles." (Psalm 2:1–3)

God can change any nation in a day. That is nothing for God. Throughout the days ahead, I continued to pray for peace. I wanted God's peace for this city, for this country. And for God to change the least likely nation toward Him. Quickly, we began to witness God's immeasurable favor.

MQM—January 18, 2012

At noon, we headed into the peak of rush hour for Karachi toward the Mutthaida Quami Movement's (MQM) headquarters. We were escorted by a screeching police car with armed officers waving off the vehicles who attempted to squeeze into the motorcade. We landed in a safely guarded portion of the city. We became reaquainted with the party members who had attended the reception the night before and met the members who had not attended.

MQM was founded by Altar Hussein, who was not present at the compound. He is currently living in London for his protection to avoid any assassination attempts. He formed this political party in hopes of giving minority groups a voice. Muslims, Buddhists, Christians, and atheists make up this group.

"Thank you, Marilyn, for loving Pakistan so much that you would choose to return for the sixth time," they all concurred. "Marilyn, would you pray for us?" Stephen and I laid hands on them, praying for each leader individually. Some had specific requests—for healing in their eyes, for diabetes, for having children.

One leader we prayed for had suffered a stroke and still didn't have full capacity on his right side. As we shared a meal together, he noticed he had been eating with his right hand, instead of his left. Praise the Lord!

Ministry Training School—January 19

Seventy stood the next day for a prayer to bear children. About twenty-eight hundred leaders gathered to learn more about the Bible, more about barren wombs that were opened because of God's faithfulness to hear the prayers of His people. I told them, "Pakistan is a favorite country of mine because you believe in prayer!" Our team showed a video clip of Lahore 2003. Some had witnessed the healings that were captured at that event, and it served to build up their faith that miracles can continue to happen today in Pakistan.

I felt impressed to teach about the four ways that Jesus heals: through His anointing, agreement in prayer, the laying on of hands, and sending the Word out through prayer. "There are miracles in your hands because of the power of God in you. All believers can pray for the sick! Mark 16 tells us to go into the world and tell the good news, and to lay hands on the sick so they will recover."

I prayed for God to encourage their faith and show them He will work through prayers. We then focused on Psalm 107:20, "He sent out His word and healed them." I asked them for all to exercise faith in what God can do, so we prayed together over the sick and prayed Scriptures over those in need of healing. Fifty stood for growths and tumors. One woman testified her tumor disappeared after three months of illness. Another woman shared that a cyst she had had for forty years was gone. Another woman had a growth on her neck that caused her to choke. She, too, was healed.

"God gives us four different ways in which He heals because God uses all of us differently. You may feel most comfortable when you pray the Word over someone. Some of you may sense His anointing and have a gift of healing. Pray for God to show you how He wants you to minister to the sick. All of us must pray for the sick as Scripture instructs us to do for one another. It's not reserved just for pastors to do or evangelists. Every believer is called to pray for those who are sick."

The power of God fell on the Pakistani people, and we thanked Him for the miracles we experienced in just a few hours. Before we closed the session, I laid hands on each leader, offering my prayers of faith over them, that God would use them in a mighty way, well past the few days of the event.

Healing Meeting, Night Sessions

I'm not sure if I've ever felt more covered in prayer than on this particular trip to Pakistan. When we arrived at the YMCA ground, the streets were lined with colorfully decorated buses transporting local attendees. Some carried up to seventy passengers inside and an additional fifty daring travelers on the roofs.

Police escorts weaved through the crowds monitoring safety. As I made my way toward the platform, a human pathway of praying believers with outstretched hands covered me. As I prepared to speak, I received a report that the attendance exceeded ninety thousand, and thousands more were waiting to get in.

As the Pakistani drums pulsated with sounds of praise, I prayed over the salvation cards that came to the platform. Testimonies of healing continued to be reported: a boy healed of stuttering, a young girl healed of demon possession, a baby born mute began to speak. We knew the power of prayer filled the stadium. I prayed for illnesses that the Holy Spirit impressed upon me to mention: back problems, infertility, tumors, eyesight, even missing eyes, chronic pain. . . . Stephen began moving around among the crowds, listening to testimonies and praying for the people. I told them to keep checking their bodies for healing, as sometimes it is a process. One man who had asked for prayer the previous night for a growth on his face said that healing had come in the night and the tumor drained. All the swelling—gone.

The ministry provided large jumbo screens to be placed outside the grounds, so those on top of buses who didn't get in could hear and see us. Our small team left in a small car and onlookers watched us leave, but the sea of people parted like the Jordan River so we could safely drive through.

Sunday Celebration

The encouragement God placed in our path through each of the day sessions and each nightly meeting set our hearts soaring toward God's goodness. We set aside time on Sunday to celebrate the stories of healing that continued to flood the platform. Dr. Paul Bhatti, slotted as the guest speaker, shared a story of how God called him to the Pakistani people. "I did not want to come here from Italy, where I practiced pediatrics and cosmetic surgery. But God called me here. . . . I felt like He was asking me to leave paradise and accept the position of prime minister here in a place of torment. The former prime minister, Shahbaz Bhatti, was gunned down outside his home in Islamabad, March 2011. This Christian man was my brother . . . I'm here because of his faith. I'm so grateful for Marilyn's prayers for our country, for the healing that's happening right now in our country, from sickness, poverty, and terrorism."

Humbly, I listened to his testimony and the legacy of his family. I thanked God for sending others to Pakistan, for the healing He had done in the few days we had together, and the healing that would continue through the prayers of His people and the Pakistani people.

Stephen met with the governor of Sindh province, Dr. Ishrat Ul Ebad Khan, prior to the event, and he promised support for our event. We received word on the last day that he wanted us to come to his residence to thank us for coming.

I had the privilege of meeting his lovely wife and prayed for his family. And before we left, we all joined hands and prayed for the country of Pakistan. Before we left, Dr. Khan graciously took me aside and said, "I'd like to be your friend. Can I text you?" This request touched me deeply. The favor I received in such a short time once again blew me away.

We then had to rush out to the last nightly event and our ministry partners helped to provide more than 150 buses to transport attendees. To see them all coming in for the last night showed the tremendous favor of the event.

I wanted to leave these people with hope, so I shared Luke 8:43: "A woman in the crowd had suffered for twelve years with constant bleeding, and she could find no cure. . . . She was a woman in a hopeless situation. But she reached out to Jesus in faith. Jesus felt the healing power of God flow out of him and he asked, 'Who touched me?' Well the disciples knew the crowd was pressing into Jesus and they couldn't tell. But then she stepped forward, trembling. She confessed she'd been healed immediately. Jesus knows when we have no hope. He is our hope. There is hope for the hopeless."

We then moved into a time of praying for skin conditions, bone issues, more tumors and growths, paralysis. A young man with crutches who had epilepsy had fallen and broken his hip bone. He dropped his crutches and boldly walked across the stage that night.

We did take up an offering at the end of the three days because we wanted to teach the people about sowing seeds of generosity. God asks us to give and He promises a return. The return isn't always financial; sometimes it's restored health, connecting with the right person, a new opportunity. My motivation to ask them to give was so they could continue to walk in blessing, and giving is a part of worship. Our team did not take the money back with us; we sowed it back into the country. More healings, and more of an outpouring of His Spirit proved to be on the people. Everything! Everything, we had hoped He made happen beyond what we could have asked or imagined.

As our flight took off, I was bursting with gratitude for all God did, surpassing all of our expectations. I smiled thinking of some of the earlier thoughts that had tried to distract me from the blessing of the days we had there in Pakistan. A record number of attendees came—the first night, 90,000, then growing to more than 210,000 on the last night. The *Christian Post* reported that 400,000 Muslims were exposed to the healing power of Jesus Christ.

It's hard to even raise the question of what's next. I know it isn't about the numbers alone, that was all God's doing. And I don't feel pressure to top or outdo one even from the next. I think of the underground church in Iran when only a few gather. Both opportunities are from God's favor, and the one touched matters to Jesus just as much as the multitude. Despite the crises and factions of radical Muslims killing Christians, we witnessed strong political parties working for peace. They don't want their nation to go under. They want to have peace. And surprisingly, thousands weren't afraid to come to the event in the midst of serious religious tension.

We heard a statistic that reportedly 13 percent of Pakistan's population is Christian. I don't go in there thinking I can convert them—only the Holy Spirit can do that. Rather I go there to give them an encounter with Jesus. I've visited about 124 countries, and Pakistan continues to draw me back. I will never forget this event; it fuels my prayers to ask God for more favor to keep on building bridges through the healing power of Jesus Christ. I live with the tension of wanting to be led by God and not letting ambition drive me.

Looking Back on the Ground Covered

Every Muslim country is a little different in its scope and expression of Islam. For example, Turkey is quite cosmopolitan. People eat pork, shop on the Sabbath, and drink alcohol during Ramadan, which is light years away from, say, Iran. Pakistan, on the other hand, is somewhere in the middle. But even that is turning now. The Pakistanis are becoming less tolerant of the United States and more radical views are rising up. With that, humanitarian projects are becoming all the more difficult. Though the extremist regime is growing, religious freedom is actually a part of their constitution. Yet it is hard to perceive this when you see the bombed-out areas and the continued persecution of Christians and Jews. Many who have helped us later died as martyrs in the process of building relationships.

Pakistan is deeply spiritually minded, moreso than the United States. There may be no other country in the world that believes in prayer more than Pakistan—devout Muslims pray five times a day. Prayer is a big part of the fabric of their world-view. Pakistanis don't have a problem believing Jesus heals—they recognize Jesus' healing power but do not view him as God. So they welcome very much any offer for prayer. From the poorest to the highest official, I've yet to have someone turn me down for prayer, especially prayers for healing.

Over my six visits to Pakistan, I have noticed a pattern emerge. The first night, people are healed of things like headaches, stomach problems, and minor ailments. But as faith builds, the miracles increase, and people are healed of more severe illnesses. I remember some of the miracles we celebrated then, too. A woman healed from twenty years of demon possession. I'll never forget one man who couldn't stop jumping up and down because he was healed from chronic back pain. And then I remember I watched an imam in Rawalpindi receive sight. He had a crazed look. He stood up and spoke slowly, and you could tell he was shell-shocked. He said, "I'm an imam and I can see now and Jesus healed me."

I remember one trip when Sarah came with me. She had just gotten married, so that trip holds fond memories for me, as we ministered together. I believe we had favor because we were just a couple of women, non-threatening. Sarah had to adjust to all the gender faux pas. Jobs that are genderless here in the States are viewed very differently there. For example, all of the caterers who baked the naan bread we served for a meal were male. A kind pat on the shoulder of a male-translator is unacceptable. Sarah honestly questioned, "Mom, many have failed in reaching out to Pakistan. What do I know about how to reach them?" During the nightly events, some came to throw rocks at us, but we kept telling them about the love of Jesus. Sarah felt impressed by the Holy Spirit to really pray for peace. By the last night, all the harassment stopped. A blanket of peace covered the meeting.

Looking back, perhaps 2005 held the greatest threat we had

yet experienced, but despite the dangers it was God's timing. At first, all seemed to be going well, even in the post-9/11 world. For the first session, Islamabad was filled with the power of God and supernatural healings. Thousands trusted for their salvation in Jesus Christ. We built strong relationships with the Catholic community there, too.

More than fifteen denominations gathered in unity to hear teaching on miracles and the ministry of the Holy Spirit. And then we learned of the threats—a terrorist cell in Pakistan planned to assassinate me. City officials found posters on the terrorists' planning table of me; Stephen; my camera man, Joe; and Robinson, the chairman of the event, with red Xs on our faces. They also marked five Xs on the stadium blueprints to show their plan of attack. The event had to be cancelled from Cricket Stadium due to the risk involved. Bin Laden had been watching us, and the setbacks were becoming so discouraging.

But God provided another venue. A charismatic Catholic church in Rawalpindi offered to host the remaining days. And once again, the Lord performed miracles of healing. Rawalpindi is like the sister city to Islamabad—Rawalpindi is where the common people live and Islamabad is sort of like Washington, D.C., full of diplomats. But Rawalpindi is important because it supports its sister city. As you walk among the people, you hear things like, "I'm here because I'm Muslim and my clergy won't pray for me." And as we continued to go back in, our history with the people grew stronger. Stephen often hears from city officials as they meet to discuss our intent, "I was at the event ten years ago. You can trust these people. They do what they say they are going to do."

I've always traveled light. I don't bring a big entourage with me. Stephen and I bring as few people with us as possible, due to the danger involved. I don't get to have as much contact with the crowds as Stephen does. He walks freely among them during an event. He believes it is a part of his commission, and his desire is to personally connect to the attendees. When security warns him against it, he shrugs it off and says, "No, I'm going." Stephen saw a man fall over and he went to pick him up. The body guards tried to stop him, but he wanted to show the man he wasn't afraid and that he truly loved him. Stephen is fully aware that as he walks among them, a man next to him could be wired to blow himself up, but this doesn't stop him. He refuses to let fear be a barrier between him and the people who come. He, too, will often say, "I love Muslims." This blows them away, as they don't understand how that can be in light of history.

As Stephen takes time to prayerfully walk through the crowds of people, it gives him a chance to ask, "Why are you here?" Some say, "I come to hear the beautiful music." Others say, "I hear this woman will pray for my healing" or "We need healing and we know Jesus heals." We always try to stop and shake as many hands as we can. When you see the needs of the young, the elderly, the young mothers, you realize the most powerful thing to do is pray, always pray.

Even when the venue had to change and government security refused to protect us because of the risk, we knew we were meant to be there. When we realized we were on a hit list, we knew our dependence on God had to be stronger than anything else. Each incident and every mile has been worth it all. And He has been watching over every event and every opportunity we've had to build a relationship that honors humanity.

IO

the heart of a humanitarian

The generous soul will be made rich,
And he who waters will also be watered himself.

—PROVERBS 11:25 NKJV

Picture what it would be like to live in the aftermath of your own consumption, never removing trash from your home. I've walked with citizens of Garbage City, a city just outside of Cairo in Egypt. The streets and buildings are piled high with rubbish— plastic, paper, waste materials, and rotting food. The stench is indescribable. Donkey-pulled carts carry garbage loads stacked up eight feet high for the Zabbaleen people, or the garbage collectors.

The sixty-five thousand residents who live in Garbage City are mostly Coptic Christians and Muslims. Illiteracy is high, particularly among women. Garbage is literally their income. Children as young as nine collect garbage in the morning. The garbage is sorted, recycled, and consumed. Then what is left is burned as fuel. Sometimes this city doesn't have running water, and the city struggles with high rates of disease due to unsanitary conditions.

Unoccupied space and vacant buildings are given to livestock, who also feed on the garbage. But within the city's trash-cluttered walls, there is life and human dignity.

I had the opportunity to sit down and talk with some Muslim women in Garbage City. "Can I pray with you?" Of course, I wasn't surprised they agreed. How easy it is to turn away from the pain we see in a fallen world. God wants us to carry the burdens of the sick, the poor, and the afflicted. We aren't the one who can fix a life, but we can go to God on someone's behalf in prayer, knowing God has the answer. Not only are we to meet spiritual needs, but we are to meet physical needs, the ones God places in our path.

Proverbs 28:27 says, "He who gives to the poor will lack nothing, but he who closes his eyes to them receives many curses" (NIV1984). It is so easy to say, "I cannot afford to give to any humanitarian relief. I have no extra. But if I were rich, I'd . . ." Statistics reveal that Americans who live at poverty level actually give more to their church than those who have more wealth. Jesus observed those bringing their offerings at the Temple court, including many wealthy people, but He took note of the widow's mite:

> Jesus sat down opposite the place where the offerings were put and watched the crowd putting their money into the temple treasury. Many rich people threw in large amounts. But a poor widow came and put in two very small copper coins, worth only a few cents.
>
> Calling his disciples to him, Jesus said, "Truly I tell you, this poor widow has put more into the treasury than all the others. They all gave out of their wealth; but she, out of her poverty, put in everything—all she had to live on." (Mark 12:41–43)

We are not told how God chose to bless this widow's offering, but it was her act of worship to God that displayed extravagant sacrifice. She put in two of the smallest coins that were in circulation in Palestine, which was all she had. To give out of one's poverty is entirely different from giving out of abundance. She gave the money she needed to live on. Her giving attitude exposed her love for God. If we waited until helping a neighbor fit into our budget, most likely most of us wouldn't give to someone in need. I want my giving to expose my love for God and to fulfill what He asks of me: "Love your neighbor as yourself." And I believe sometimes that means giving when it isn't convenient or easy.

No one of us can wipe out world hunger, but whatever we are able to do does make a difference, which is why the widow's mite is so encouraging. Jesus didn't scoff at the small amount, but He saw it from the kingdom perspective—God blesses a generous heart. I also believe that God multiplies what we give. If we don't give, plant a seed of generosity, then nothing can grow into a harvest. He makes it go farther than we can. Most Americans can make some changes for the better to help transform society. We can help some of the poor get on their feet and develop a skill set. We can provide clean water for some who do not have it in third world countries. We can fight against prejudices in our communities that oppress the poor, the uneducated, or the immigrant.

Helping a country or people group in need, I believe, is a biblical mandate, but I also believe those who do not embrace Christianity can agree that there is something morally right about it, though perhaps a non-Christian wouldn't point to Scripture in drawing the same conclusion. I believe it is inherently in all of us to give to others.

When I heard about the devastating earthquake of 2005, my heart went out to the Pakistani people, both Christians and Muslims. I wanted to know the details, so the ministry quickly began investigating. Our connections with leaders in Karachi helped us to send relief quickly, and the governor kept us informed. Approximately 74,000 people died and 106,000 were injured. For days and weeks following, the villages were trapped in the rubble, waiting to be rescued. Our ministry felt led to help provide relief to survivors. The money we sent helped with food, water, and bedding supplies. We also supported a school that served earthquake victims in a Hindu community.

Pakistan faced another devastating natural disaster in 2010, a flood that impacted 20 million people, leaving many homeless. Two thousand lives were taken, and more than four hundred health care facilities were destroyed. Through the years, I've continued to stay connected with Pakistan, so when the news hit the airwaves, our team felt the call to send help. Sometimes you wonder: how much tragedy can one country survive? And yet, the Pakistani people continue to press on, through natural disasters, oppressive regimes, and poverty. I also felt the mandate to encourage, so we translated some of my teaching resources into Urdu. I try to follow Jesus' example of meeting physical needs as well as spiritual needs.

In a greedy world, sometimes we think it is justified to hold a tight fist to what is ours and look away from the needs of a friend or neighbor. What does greed look like in a modern context? Usually we don't have to look too far to see evidence of greed where we live, whether we live in an affluent neighborhood or in the slums of the inner city. Greed often stems from how we view God and how we value others.

For the past forty years, Eunice Pike has worked with the Mazatec Indians in southwestern Mexico. During this time she has discovered some interesting things about these beautiful people. For instance, the people seldom wish someone well. Not only that, they are hesitant to teach one another or to share the gospel with each other. If asked, "Who taught you to bake bread?" the village baker answers, "I just know," meaning he has acquired the knowledge without anyone's help. Eunice says this odd behavior stems from the Indians' concept of "limited good." They believe there is only so much good, so much knowledge, so much love to go around. To teach another means you might drain yourself of knowledge. To love a second child means you have to love the first child less. To wish someone well, to say something as simple as "Have a good day," means giving away some of your *own* happiness, which cannot be reacquired.

One American poll asked, What would you be willing to do for ten million dollars? Two-thirds of those polled agreed to at least one, some to several of the following:

Would abandon their entire family (25%)
Would abandon their church (25%)
Would become prostitutes for a week or more (23%)
Would give up their American citizenships (16%)
Would leave their spouses (16%)
Would withhold testimony and let a murderer go free (10%)
Would kill a stranger (7%)
Would put their children up for adoption (3%)

Greed says, "It's never enough." Have you ever felt that way? Somehow that long-awaited raise doesn't ever seem to provide the extra we thought it would. Nothing quite feeds our appetite to consume when life is only about fulfilling self. The Bible does give examples of greed that might reflect the results of the poll: Laban cheated Jacob from wages and the wife he was promised; Lot took his uncle's wealth and left his family; Ananias and Sapphira stole from their church, and ultimately from God.

In contrast, we see ample examples of generous people throughout the Bible. Abraham gave his nephew Lot whatever he wanted in the way of land and his wealth. Boaz took Ruth, a poor widow, as his wife, along with her mother-in-law. Job, a wealthy man, told God to curse him if he denied the desires of the poor or let the eyes of the widow grow weary, or if he kept his bread to himself, not sharing it with the fatherless—if he saw anyone perishing for lack of clothing, a needy man without a garment. Rather than being someone who looked away from the needs of the poor, Job asked for a curse.

Jesus continually looked to the needs of the poor during his ministry. He identified with them. Philippians 2 tells us Jesus emptied Himself of His rightful throne to come to earth as a man, where He was born in a feeding trough to a couple who had no wealth to offer the Son of God. He then earned wages as a carpenter and died on the Cross with common criminals. His own town rejected his ministry, and the religious leaders He came to save gave him an unjust trial and sentenced Him to death. He understood the pain and suffering of an unjust world. The late John Stott, renowned evangelical leader, said it well: "I could never myself believe in God if it were not for the Cross. In the real world of pain, how could one worship a God who was immune to it?"

Throughout history, scholars, lay people, and seekers of Truth have asked, "Why did Jesus have to die?" I believe part of the answer is right here when we look at how Jesus "emptied" Himself of all He deserved. Humanity needed a God who understood what it was like to be rejected, despised, and impoverished. He stood in our place on the Cross, took on our spiritual poverty, and bore it Himself. That's why Jesus said, "I tell you the truth, whatever you did for one of the least of these brothers of mine, you did for me." He identified with the marginalized, though He was God. Some use human suffering as a reason to deny God's existence. Yet Jesus addressed it firsthand and experienced injustice in the most radical way, spiritually and physically, in part so that He could identify with us and with every kind of human suffering.

As I reflect on my worldview, I see the beauty of God's plan, though the Cross is scandalous and continues to be a stumbling block to many people. If an Infinite God stooped to be among His Creation in such a tangible way, to serve and sacrifice as He did, then I should all the more co-labor with Him to follow His example in how to love others.

I believe the majority of people on the planet, whether Christian, Muslim, Hindu, or declared atheist, desire peace. In his book, *A Generous Justice,* Timothy Keller challenges the reader to do as Micah 6:8 says, "to live justly, love mercy, and walk humbly with God," and this leads to *shalom.* Usually we define *shalom* to mean "peace." But the meaning has a larger context—it really means "complete reconciliation." When a neighborhood is infested with crime and innocent children are gunned down, there is no shalom. When there is a breakdown of the family, there is no shalom. But when we work together and share resources, a community can be restored and God can take our offering and show us that justice can abound in the darkest corners.

I've seen this principle at work over and over again. "He who sows generously will reap generously." Whatever it is you do to the least of these, you can be certain God will match your efforts because of His generosity. I remember a time early in my marriage. Wally and I didn't have much money and we traveled a lot; wherever God wanted us to go and preach, we told Him we'd go. We weren't sure if we'd get one more mile out of our car, but we were trying to get it to last as long as possible. I had been saving a little bit here and there so we could buy a more reliable used car. Then Wally felt impressed to give to a ministry in a very lavish way—he put in the offering all we had. I couldn't believe he did that! I was angry and didn't think that was wise at all. But then, miraculously, God gave us a car far better than what my small savings could buy. He showed me, in a tangible way, how we couldn't ever out-give Him. That example has stayed with me all these years. When I find He is prompting me to give sacrificially, I know it is so He can do much more with my offering than I could ever do on my own.

> For I was hungry and you gave me something to eat, I was thirsty and you gave me something to drink, I was a

stranger and you invited me in, I needed clothes and you clothed me, I was sick and you looked after me, I was in prison and you came to visit me.'

"Then the righteous will answer him, 'Lord, when did we see you hungry and feed you, or thirsty and give you something to drink? When did we see you a stranger and invite you in, or needing clothes and clothe you? When did we see you sick or in prison and go to visit you?'

"The King will reply, 'Truly I tell you, whatever you did for one of the least of these brothers and sisters of mine, you did for me.' (Matthew 25:35–40 NIV1984)

Part II

I I

worldview: everyone has one

*He is the God who made the world and everything in it.
Since he is Lord of heaven and earth, he doesn't live in man-
made temples, and human hands can't serve his needs—for
he has no needs. He himself gives life and breath to
everything, and he satisfies every need.*

—ACTS 17:24–25 NLT

The term *worldview* is one we hear more and more. Everyone—
religious or atheist, spiritual or unspiritual—has a worldview.
Simply stated, worldview is how a person views the world. A
worldview sets out to answer the questions Who am I? Why am
I here? How did we get here? Who is God? The goal is to develop a framework that makes sense of reality and how to pursue life.

You can observe and interact with a person and learn a lot
about their worldview from how they approach life and live it
out. Take, for example, a toddler. Most toddlers have a very limited perspective of the world; their tendency is to believe they are
the center. This is partially out of necessity—they depend on
their parents to meet all their needs. As a one-year-old grows and
becomes more aware of others, his world expands and he begins
to acknowledge the needs of others. It doesn't take long to figure
out how a young child views the reality around him. Though a

toddler cannot articulate what she believes, her actions tell us what is true for her scope of reality.

How we respond to suffering also illustrates how we view life and the world. For a Buddhist, to be liberated from suffering means to pursue self-purification, which involves following an eight-fold path, which leads to a state of nirvana or enlightenment. A Buddhist believes that suffering is caused by the afflicted person. Buddha said, "I teach one thing and one thing only: suffering and the end of suffering." A Christian, on the other hand, points to several things that can cause suffering: sin, the consequences of living in a fallen world, the presence of Satan. A Christian's first response is usually to pray and ask God to direct him or her toward healing or relief. God is the ultimate source of power and wisdom, so apart from God suffering is meaningless.

For the Christian, all suffering has the ability to grow us in our faith, and it can also be used to bring God glory in specific ways. For example, when I witnessed the healing of a blind child in Pakistan, I knew that God had heard our prayers for healing. I believe in the healing power of Jesus, and I knew where the healing had come from. We all prayed as the Holy Spirit led us to pray, but no one can take credit for the healing, because all of us praying knew it was God's healing touch that gave sight to the child. For the Christian, this suffering turns to a testimony of victory, God's authority over humanity is displayed and His glory can be tangibly seen. My response to suffering is driven by my Christian worldview, so I see suffering very differently than a Buddhist does.

Worldview matters because it is what we believe to be true, so it drives our decisions, our emotions, and our responses to all of life. A biblical worldview finds truth about the world from God. Scripture tells us where we came from, who we are, and that we all have a purpose in this life. If you follow theories of evolution, then you accept that the big bang happened and we come from primordial soup. There isn't an Intelligent Designer or a Creator behind our existence. And as you follow that framework, the assumptions lead to a belief that life is about cosmic chance, not purposeful, loving design by the power of a Loving God.

I believe that Christianity really is the only worldview that answers all of the hard questions. I don't mean to say that we don't have to wrestle with why things happen or that we can fully understand an Infinite God. But I do believe it provides us with a clear guide to life, and that the Creator of the Universe wants to have daily communion with humanity. When we follow Him, He will guide us and give us the answers we need to live in times of trials, testing, and suffering as well as success and seasons of blessing.

The Christian and Jewish worldviews are the only systems of belief that acknowledge sin. Both acknowledge that we were created in a state of perfection and Adam and Eve were God's most treasured creations. But Adam and Eve were deceived by the Deceiver and sinned against God.

Other worldviews deny our need for salvation and turn toward the idea that everyone is inherently good. But as we experience the world—as we read the headlines, see the outbreaks of violence in our communities, hear rumors of war, and witness the rise in prison populations, sin is an undeniable fact.

A biblical worldview informs us about every aspect of life and is efficient for all we need in life and practice. I like the framework Chuck Colson used to discuss a Christian worldview in his book *How Shall We Then Live?*—Creation, Fall, Redemption, and Restoration.

Creation

A Christian worldview really begins with the Creation story. We are created in the image of God. Whether a person acknowledges it or not, Scripture tells us that we bear His image. The Apostle Paul appealed to Scripture all the time when addressing those he met on his missionary journeys. But it's interesting to note how we see Paul understand the worldview of those in Athens. He tells them that they have a Creator that can be known. Acts 17 says:

> Paul then stood up in the meeting of the Areopagus and said: "People of Athens! I see that in every way you are very religious. For as I walked around and looked carefully at your objects of worship, I even found an altar with this inscription: TO AN UNKNOWN GOD. So you are ignorant of the very thing you worship—and this is what I am going to proclaim to you.
>
> "The God who made the world and everything in it is the Lord of heaven and earth and does not live in temples built by human hands. And he is not served by human hands, as if he needed anything. Rather, he himself gives everyone life and breath and everything else. From one man he made all the nations, that they should inhabit the whole earth; and he marked out their appointed times in history and the boundaries of their lands. God did this so that they would seek him and perhaps reach out for him and find him, though he is not far from any one of us. 'For in him we live and move and have our being.' As some of your own poets have said, 'We are his offspring.'
>
> "Therefore since we are God's offspring, we should not think that the divine being is like gold or silver or stone— an image made by human design and skill. In the past God overlooked such ignorance, but now he commands all people everywhere to repent. For he has set a day when he will judge the world with justice by the man he has ap-

pointed. He has given proof of this to everyone by raising him from the dead." (Acts 17:22–31)

In this passage, Paul addresses the Athens audience, acknowledging that he understands their beliefs about idols, and says he sees how they are religious people. He points to the altar he observed that said, "to an unknown god." He presents to the crowd a Christian worldview, a God who is personal and can be known, a knowable God who gives life and we are His offspring. Paul grasped the need to understand the worldview around him, a worldview that indeed clashed with his biblical worldview.

Worldview is often a logical starting point. When we reach out to a neighbor or someone from a different religious background, it is important for that person to believe that we are aware of his or her worldview. If we don't seek to understand or know what someone believes, there is more room for misunderstanding, and stereotypes can take over, resulting in a wedge. I believe this is why Paul started with the people of Athens' worldview. He met them where they were first and took them toward a God who could be known, a God who created them.

Fall

The Fall of humanity recorded in Genesis 3 is what answers the question, *What went wrong with the world?* When Adam and Eve sinned, they were kicked out of paradise because they disobeyed God and listened to the Deceiver, Satan. Their sin caused a rift in their relationship with God, and God declared a curse over Adam and Eve as well as the serpent. Even the created order was impacted by the Fall. In our postmodern world, sin is a very unpopular doctrine. It's popular to view humanity as basically "good." This view of humanity allows for someone to say, "I don't need a Savior. I try to be kind and do the right things. I'm not an evil person." Most Americans would fall into this category. But I believe that to ignore our sinful nature is to leave us vulnerable and unprepared for what we are capable of doing apart from God. Undeniably, the effects of sin are all around us. Most of us can see clear evidence of it in our daily family life.

Redemption

The next important part of a Christian worldview points to redemption—the solution for sin. Jesus Christ. Sin had to be appeased by a Holy God and Jesus' death, burial, and resurrection took care of all our sin so that we might become righteous again. In other words, Jesus restored us back to our pre-Fall standing with God. Only Jesus could save humanity because He was fully man and fully God.

Christianity is the only worldview that claims to have a Savior from sin. It is also the only worldview that is based upon a relationship of grace. Grace is a gift from God; it cannot be earned. Sometimes even Christians fall into a works mentality, but Scripture is clear. We cannot bridge the gap of sin between us and God—Jesus is that bridge. When someone repents and acknowledges her need for a Savior, she's given freedom and sin no longer controls her because of the work of the Cross and the power of the Holy Spirit at work that indwells this new believer. *Redeem* really means "to save." And for those who place their trust in Jesus Christ, that means a soul is saved from death, sin, and giving eternal life.

This would clash with the Muslim understanding of salvation. For a Muslim, salvation is something you earn, so no one is certain he is saved until death. One tradition (hadith) says "Allah has ninety-nine names, and whoever knows them will go to Paradise." A Muslim won't know if he is saved from hell or not until the final judgment. While Muslims have a concept of sin, it is more reflective of an individual's act of disobedience to God rather than a condition. They think: Adam disobeyed God, but more from ignorance and forgetfulness, not rebellion.

Restoration

The Christian believes that the kingdom can be here and now. Once a believer is following God, there is a desire to share the Gospel. Salvation isn't a private matter to be hoarded, but rather it is for the benefit of others personally and also is a tool to transform culture.

If you look at Christians who have impacted our society, it is overwhelming what their love for Christ has done. For example, Chuck Colson spent about forty years of his life spreading hope to incarcerated people. Chuck's conversion experience happened before he went to prison, when a friend witnessed to him and gave him a copy of *Mere Christianity* by C. S. Lewis. After serving seven months in prison, Chuck found a new purpose in life and Prison Fellowship was later established. Chuck Colson realized that reform in prison was essential to restore a man or woman back into society.

William Wilberforce, a member of the British Parliament, used his platform to abolish slavery, the social ill of his country during the nineteenth century. As a man of prayer, he committed this huge political and economic evil of his day to God and transformed his country. Amidst much opposition, Wilberforce continued to present bills to the British Parliament from 1791 to the very end of his life, and in 1833, a month after his death, slavery was abolished.

Mother Teresa believed she was called by God to love humanity. She felt particularly called to the poorest of the poor in Calcutta, where she shared the love of Christ, washing the sores on the sick, bathing children, and nursing those dying of hunger. By 1997, Mother Teresa had trained more than four thousand nuns to serve in missionary work. She would say it was Christ's love that compelled her to go Calcutta.

Life takes on purpose when we believe that God has given us an assignment. I believe each person has immeasurable value when he or she submits to God's plan. Life has meaning now, and I don't believe I have to wait until heaven to experience God's kingdom among us. A worldview should be able to make sense of life, of why we are here and where we are headed.

For me, this goes back to why I do what I do. To strive to be the greatest humanitarian is not my goal. To be a renowned teacher is not my goal. I believe I'm called to share the love of Christ to those in oppressed countries and to go until He tells me otherwise. And as I look at the world around me, the Muslim people have suffered a great deal through oppressive regimes. I do have a biblical mandate to reach out to the poor, and to overlook Muslim countries is to overlook the poor. With God's guidance, it really is possible to love someone with an opposing worldview. Relationships can be built on mutual respect and love. In the midst of differences and different beliefs about who God is, honesty and friendship are great ways to build a bridge. But without His guidance, His Hand upon me, it really becomes just about works. So I pray that I live out my Christian worldview in a way that honors others and makes them curious about a Savior who heals.

12

dialogue with a muslim

We want the peace of the brave for our children and for their children, for a bright future where they can live and learn.

—Yasser Arafat

Not all Muslims express their faith in the same way, but stereotypes have led us to believe they do. Some hold onto identifying with Islam to honor family tradition. Others are cultural Muslims who grew up embracing this expression of faith but are not practicing. In speaking to American Muslims and Muslims from other countries, the understanding of Islam varies. Some believe Islam promotes peace and acceptance according to what they believe the Quran teaches; others have never read the Quran but identify as Muslim out of loyalty.

One Muslim family I've grown to love is the Nouri family. I've been able to get to know David and his sister, Tara, over the past few years. We've shared family dinners and even holidays together, with many opportunities to discuss God, share our struggles, and pray together. Though I know they are Muslim, I love it when I get to see them at church. I just keep inviting them any chance I get, and they do come.

David and his family moved to America when he was two years old, so his memories of Iran come from conversations with his grandfather and his parents. The Nouri family worked for the government. During the revolution, they fled due to persecution. One of David's uncles served in Tehran as the chief of police and helped the family come to America. As a child, David spent a lot of time with his grandfather, who was a devout Muslim. He watched his grandfather stop throughout the day to take out his beads and pray. David wasn't allowed to interrupt his call to prayer and was expected to wait patiently for him to finish. Though he grew up in America, David learned to read and write in Farci. David, now in his early thirties, considers himself to be Muslim, but not practicing. He says, "I definitely believe in God, but I didn't grow up in a religious home. If I did convert to Christianity, a part of me feels like I would be betraying my ancestors and, more specifically, my grandfather."

As I mentioned in chapter 6, I used David's transportation service to the airport. When I first met him, I asked about his nationality. "We are Greek," he said. Later, I learned that he and his family were actually Persian, but he feared I'd be prejudiced if I knew they were Muslims from the Middle East.

Tara, his younger sister, worked for her brother's transportation business for a time, and I met her soon after I met David. She, too, has attended our church and we've had some Bible studies together. Tara shared with me that she hasn't ever read the Quran but does read her Bible. So whenever I get a chance, I encourage her to read a Scripture and stay connected to us at church.

One day, I said to her, "Tara, do you remember when you came to the airport with those beautiful flowers for me on Mother's Day? That was just so sweet and I'll never forget it."

"Yes, I remember. My brother and I consider you to be like a mother to us. You've taught us a lot about God and who Jesus is."

"Well, you need to get back to church," I teased.

"Yes, I know. It always makes me feel better when I go. . . . You helped me through that tough relationship I had, and I was able to let go of it and move on."

"You know I love you, Tara. Tonight I want you to read Psalm 139. God is closer than you think."

"Okay, I will. Sometimes when I'm having a bad day and I get down, I just question if God is real. Like, I want him to show Himself to me in a real way. I believe in God, and Mom and Dad never forced us to be Muslim. They want us to choose for ourselves what we believe. I just sometimes wish He'd show me who He is in a more tangible way. Most Christians I've met say, they've had an experience that has brought them closer to God—I haven't had that yet."

"Well, come to church on Sunday," I suggested. "I saw David last Sunday, and he looks so good; I met his girlfriend. And before you go to bed, read Psalm 139."

"Okay, Marilyn, I will. Love you, bye!"

Both Tara and David have professed belief in God, and during our conversations we have talked about the different views I have about Jesus Christ, that He is Savior and not just a prophet like the Quran teaches. Not only is He healer, but He is Savior. In attending our church, David says he's learned more about Jesus that he did not know before. We keep talking, keep encouraging one another, and I want them to know I'm here for them.

The Nouri siblings are still searching for answers about God, and I'm glad they are encouraged when they come to church. I love to answer their questions about the Bible. The core beliefs of Islam aren't guiding their spiritual life, though the label "Muslim" is something they still identify with as a part of their heritage. I'm grateful they allow me to share the hope I have for them. As Paul prayed, I pray that the eyes of their heart would be enlightened in order that they'd know the hope He is calling them to know (Ephesians 1:18). I'll never stop encouraging them to come to church! I cherish my conversations with both of them.

Imam Elahi and his wife, Jennifer, have a passion to continue to dialogue with other faith traditions and are deeply committed to gathering others around the table at the Islamic House of Wisdom. Jennifer understands the Christian worldview well, having grown up in a Catholic home. She knows what the theological tensions are, but she desires to live out her Muslim worldview seeking relationships with those who worship God differently than her family. Jennifer's conversion story is another example of how American Muslims differ in practice and belief.

Jennifer's Story

"I grew up in Catholic home and attended catechism. My family went to church occasionally, but not as much as I wanted. As a child, I always felt a strong connection with faith, but I was searching for more than what was taught in my catechism book. In my high school years, I spent every chance I had studying comparative faith. After four years of research, I found the path I should take—Islam. During the summer of 2001, I focused my research on Muslim worship in mosques. It was after 9/11 when I took a leap of faith and attended my first mosque service. Growing up in the country, I wasn't exposed to other faith traditions, let alone other cultures. But I found it comforting to find the first Muslims I met to be welcoming and inviting. From this experience, I became involved in the local Muslim community activities. I found that the outreach experiences paralleled my Christian experience, and my heritage made the transition add to the faith I already had.

"When I married Imam Elahi, we shared the same passion for youth. Most every faith realizes that they are not exempt from losing youth to drugs, alcohol, violence, and sex. Parents are burying their children, and children are raising their parents. Through social networking, religious services, and outreach in the community, we are trying to connect. I recently heard that the church I grew up in cut their youth program. I told my husband that it hurts deeply to hear this, no matter what faith, to see people lose opportunities to connect with God. Recently, I reached out to my childhood parish, to open up a dialogue, to see how we might reflect on our strengths and weaknesses to reach the youth.

"I wish there was an immediate solution to the suffering that is unavoidable. Some situations are so heartbreaking—it wears you out emotionally at times. It's easy to want to throw in the towel, to back away and live a life not caring about others. To focus on your kids and taking care of your own household sounds safer at times, less filled with heartache. But I know life wouldn't have meaning if I chose to ignore my community. And prayer keeps me going.

"A devout Muslim prays five times daily, and I find this discipline revives me when I'm weary. To submit to God's call to prayer. To do it five times a day takes discipline, obedience, humility, and understanding. During prayer time, I'm redirected as I focus on God is the Ultimate, that He is just, and loving, that He is forgiving.

Through God, I believe humanity is united and He reminds us of a call to morality and responsibility toward one another. I want to see people of faith move past labels and stereotypes and not see all Muslims as the authors of 9/11. . . . A church near our house blocks traffic a few days a week. While I want to be upset when it delays my travel time, I praise God that there are God-loving people in the world who feel a purpose and a mission under God.

Tara, David, and the Elahis are part of American Muslim families—but very different ones. If you were to follow either family around, their lived-out expressions of faith would look completely different. David says, "I'm not really religious, but I love the encouragement I receive at Marilyn's church." Tara says, "I'm more Christian than Muslim. I'm waiting on a personal encounter with God." David and Tara identify more with their ancestors, but they are not practicing Muslims like the Elahis, and they feel the freedom to seek God at a Christian church. I will never stop encouraging them to come to our church!

Imam Elahi and Jennifer continue to embrace the real differences we have, but they also honor our friendship and welcome my prayers for their family. Our relationship continues to grow. They don't want to convert me—they want me to continue to follow God's call on my life, reaching out to Muslims so they can experience the healing power of Jesus Christ. Both families respect my convictions about Jesus, that He is the Son of God, and I will teach others about His love for them till I see Him face to face. I can't stop!

I look back on shared meals, phone calls, and even times when God allowed us to pray together, and I realize that only God can open such doors and grow such friendships. My desire is to continue to extend my hand of friendship, share my faith, and let God do the rest.

13
dialogue with a skeptic

A weird time in which we are alive. We can travel anywhere we want, even to other planets. And for what? To sit day after day, declining in morale and hope.

—Philip K. Dick

Skeptics make up about 15 to 25 percent of the population of the United States. Some are atheists. Some are agnostic. For the skeptic, reality is tested through rational evidence. If there isn't enough rational, supporting evidence, the skeptic will live the matter in question. Classical philosophical skepticism was a school of thought that asserted nothing.

Naturalism points to the laws of nature and denies any supernatural existence; it's the spring board for atheism, some forms of skepticism, nihilism, and existentialism. In our pluralistic society, the worldviews we encounter are often complex. But the more we dialogue, the more we can eliminate assumptions about someone who has a different worldview.

Bill Spies, a forty-something in a committed relationship and a single father, describes himself as an atheist existentialist. Existentialism can be quite a complicated worldview because of the wide range of expressions, and it is difficult to define. The main ideas behind this system of beliefs are that our choices are the guiding force in our lives and the individual determines what to believe about reality; there is an acknowledgment that science and knowledge is limited, and experience is what shapes life, though the purpose in life cannot be known in an unfathomable universe. And that is a misery the existentialist is confronted with.

Bill describes his father as a lapsed Catholic and his mother as Pentecostal—a supporter of Jimmy Swaggart's ministry, a "Jesus Camp" kind of Christian. So Christianity is definitely something Bill experienced growing up. Bill was baptized as an infant. He even says he has tried to have faith but has determined that he isn't a spiritual person.

"There were times when I tried to have faith, but it has never been something I've been able to achieve. . . . I still believe if you are lucky enough to have faith, you will be happier. I think it gives people something to rely on. Sometimes I wish I had something like that, but I've had three surgeries in rapid succession, and they were dicey. I almost died. In dealing with Crohn's disease and cancer, it'd be nice to have faith. I'm not a spiritual person, but not happily so."

For the Christian, absolute truths are essential in embracing God's Word. For an existentialist, truth is derived from the individual and his experience of reality. Bill discusses his beliefs:

I could go on and on about, what is truth? But when I think of reality, it's what I experience. The color red isn't really red, but rather it's reflecting red, it's light waves. When I touch a table, I do believe it is really there, but I can't prove it is there. Still, it's real enough for me to accept it as my reality. So with morality, it is as real as color to me. I do believe we inherited morality, like reciprocity. Evolution has imbued us with communal survival tactics. For me that is also truth. Moral imperatives are real.

Though I don't believe in God, I don't feel like I'm free to get away with whatever. I feel it . . . know it . . . when I've done something wrong. Christianity is actually a very comforting religion, I think. You do something wrong, and there is a way to rectify it, a place for your guilt to go. You can ask for forgiveness and repent. All those things, I think can be good for a person. I personally would never talk anyone out of being a Christian.

I found Bill's honesty to be refreshing. His open posture and his responses to some of life's deepest questions showed a seeking heart for truth. Some of us aren't really looking to answer the harder realities of life. It's common to hear a statement like, "Well, I believe I'm a good person; therefore I don't believe I'm going to hell." For the Christian, we know sin is what separates us from God and Jesus is the answer to the sin issue. Sin is so profound that God sent His son to atone for our sins, so we could be saved from death. The whole topic of sin today is unpopular; we don't want to see the reality of our condition.

Bill's perspective seems to be atypical from what most nonbelievers might say about sin, suffering, and evil:

Do you believe humanity is inherently good or bad?

Well, I think they say 4 percent of the world's population are sociopaths. I'd say most of us can admit we know when we do something wrong. My girlfriend and I were watching the Biography Channel on serial killers. When someone doesn't have a conscience, you feel it—it's creepy. But back to evolution. I'd say humanity's tendency is to make bad choices, selfish choices. It's in us to try and get what we want. But the way I understand Christianity, sin is an act that separates a person from God. Well, I don't believe in God, so morality for me is different. Like, I don't think premarital sex is wrong, or I've never felt guilty for not keeping the Sabbath.

How do you view evil and suffering?

Suffering is ubiquitous. It's unavoidable. We weren't meant to be happy. Evolution only cares about reproduction. It makes more people, who just evolve into more miserable people. Really death is where we find relief. I love this quote by novelist H. P. Lovecraft: "There is nothing better than oblivion, since in oblivion there is no wish unfulfilled." (I don't think my psyche can handle immortal existence—it would drive me insane.) The constant want and need that we live with helps us survive, but it does not lead to happiness. . . . I do believe in evil, but not as in a devil, a spiritual force. Rather evil is something I can partake in naturally, a natural inclination.

Bill remembers being in his car on the way to work when hearing about the planes crashing into the Twin Towers. I just remember watching the coverage. We cancelled all meetings that day. The events of 9/11 didn't change my view of Muslims. I believe the Muslim faith had little to do with what happened. Religion often serves as a veneer for other motives. What happened that day was political, not spiritual. I'd say that Islam is no more violent than Christianity. I think you'd be hard-pressed to find a Muslim in America who felt what happened was morally right."

For Bill, humanity at its worst looks like what most every person might say: suicide bombings, racial wars, genocide, sexual abuse. He believes these universal truths are known by all of us. On the other side of the spectrum, Bill also described what humanity looks like when we are at our best: we love each other, we care for one another.

Through all the miles I've traveled in ministry, love is a force that has such power. Jesus commanded us to love one another. Though Bill admitted he doesn't really know much about Jesus, he agrees with Jesus' mandate—love one another. As a father, he knows the reward of being a parent and the love that he receives back. Though he wouldn't say parenting has given his life purpose, it is a responsibility he loves having.

For the existentialist, it is difficult to find purpose in life. In light of the non-Christian expression of existentialism, God can't be the source where a person's calling is derived. Humbly Bill admitted, "I struggle with what my purpose in life really is. I don't think I really know. Since I've been sick, I had to quit my job as a counselor. Helping kids with learning disabilities gave me a reason to get up in the morning. Then that all changed, and it's gone. I felt like I was contributing positively in others. I felt needed and useful to others. I did receive a lot of pats on the back from my job. I've found there's something beautiful about exploring the mind. I've always been fascinated with therapists. Maybe because I had no spirituality, the idea that there is a lot more going on than what I thought or perceived intrigues me. I do know this: relationships matter the most, though we may never know what the purpose of life is. "

All of humanity is searching for purpose, for ways to serve one another. Christians seek for ways to serve God and humanity. Ephesians 2:10 says, " For we are God's handiwork, created in Christ Jesus to do good works, which God prepared in advance for us to do.

The more we live for ourselves, the more miserable we become. No matter if we are an imam, a lawyer, a counselor, a teacher, I believe most of us want to contribute and add value to a society. We do have that common ground, where we can be humanitarians together. No matter how much we disagree with a certain worldview, we cannot deny the dignity of life found in the eyes of our neighbor when we sit across the table from one another and share in a discussion about life, whether we are a Christian, a Muslim, or a skeptic.

I think when we begin to ask the hard questions of life, we are confronted with, What would I die for, and who or what would I live for? For me, God continues to give me a passion to share my faith with the nations in a world where rumors of war and civil wars break out daily. To be "safe" isn't my life goal. I believe in eternal life, and I want those with an opposing worldview to know about it. I want Muslims, Jews, agnostics, atheists, to at least hear that God's grace is for everyone who believes in Him. I continue to be expectant thinking and praying about who God might place around my dinner table.

14

Q & A with marilyn

She speaks with wisdom, and faithful instruction is on her tongue.

—Proverbs 31:26

Communication and understanding are essential when we reach out to anyone who might be different from us. Proverbs 31:26 says that faithful instruction should be on our tongues. I like how the King James Version says it: "and on her tongue is the law of kindness." This is a reminder of God's standard for us. Our words and what we say should be influenced by God's law—His teachings. And when we are grappling with opposing worldviews and our differences, kindness and compassion reflect the very nature of Jesus Christ.

I've had all kinds of questions about my heart for Muslims and why I do what I do. I tried to come up with some common questions that either stop the average person from reaching out and building bridges or perhaps leave us unsure if it is safe to extend a hand of friendship. Ultimately, everyone needs to rely on the direction of the Holy Spirit. But in our times and with the changes that are happening in our country, the Muslim community continues to grow, and we need to know what we believe and why we believe it. To ignore a whole group of people is to ignore the image of God in another, and I believe the topic is becoming more and more relevant. God does have answers about how to live side by side when we have opposing worldviews.

My hope is you will find some of this honest dialogue as a way to safely press and pray through what God might be calling you to do.

Why should I reach out to Muslims?

I believe Christians should reach out to Muslims because the reality is that one-fifth of the population is Muslim. American Muslims aren't going to go away; statistically there are more than before 9/11. Is there a chance of rejection? Yes, but whatever we share, such as our love for Jesus Christ and the truth about God's grace, we have to remember it isn't our job to convert—that is the work of the Holy Spirit. So I like to tell Christians, yes, be bold and share your faith, but it isn't always our business to know what they do with that information—we may never know. I also think patience and long-term suffering are important. Relationships take time and lots of prayer.

What does the Qu'ran say about Jesus, and should I read it?

I have read the Qu'ran, and Jesus is considered to be a prophet who heals but not God and Savior. It does confirm a virgin birth but denies that Jesus was crucified and resurrected. Though Jesus is a highly revered prophet, His deity is denied. There is a lot about Abraham, Ishmael, Noah, and Moses. Interestingly enough, Mary, the mother of Jesus, is the only woman mentioned in the Qu'ran. Muslims do respect Mary because of the reverence shown to her in the Qu'ran. I don't think it is necessary to study the Qu'ran, but knowing some information about what it says about Jesus can be very helpful. I know that I've been able to find common ground through my heart to pray for healing; and Muslims very much believe Jesus heals, perhaps even more than some Christians.

What makes Christianity different from other world religions?

In traveling to more than a hundred countries and observing various world religions, I've discovered that every other system is based on works and performance. Maybe you will make it to heaven, maybe you won't. Christianity is the only worldview that provides the sacrifice and solution to sin through Jesus Christ, who suffered on the cross and rose again on the third day to atone for humanity's sin. Jesus died in our place, and so we are saved by grace and faith alone, not works (Ephesians 2:8,9). Though it is true that Christianity is considered to be a religion, it is different from all other religions because it really is a relationship with the Trinity—Father, Son, and Holy Spirit. Without Jesus Christ, I have no way to the Father, but salvation provides this. Christians do not have to wonder if they are going to heaven—they can have the assurance of their salvation. And not only do we have eternal life, we have been given the right to have intimacy with the Father. John 17:1–3 is Jesus' prayer that we would be one with the Godhead, Father, Son, and Holy Spirit. That He desires such intimacy with us is a blessing that is not to be overlooked. We now come boldly to the throne room of grace because He has lavishly provided the way to the Father, Son, and Holy Spirit.

Most of us want to believe we are inherently good. But anything good comes from God, so we cannot rely on ourselves for our goodness to pave the way to salvation. I don't believe anyone can save themselves from sin. Scripture says, "the heart is intensely wicked" (Jeremiah 17:17). All of us fall short and miss the standard God has for us. Romans 3:23 also says we've all fallen short of the glory of God. But we can confidently rely on the saving work of Jesus and know that His grace is more than enough.

I also believe that Christianity is the only faith tradition that has answers to what every worldview tries to answer: Why am I here? What's my purpose, and what has gone wrong with the world? God Himself gives us purpose and all of us have a calling that He wants us to live out, as He prepared good works in advance for us to do (Ephesians 2:10).

How do I reach out to Muslims in my community?

I have found Muslim people to be friendly. Women who wear the head coverings can make us look away, and for whatever reasons we convince ourselves that they aren't approachable. My experience has proven that quite the opposite is true. It's easier to know if a woman is Muslim because of the dress, so Muslim men aren't as easily identifiable and may just appear foreign if you do not converse and find out what they believe. Muslims in general are social and responsive to friendship. Perhaps you know of a Muslim family in your neighborhood or you've noticed a Muslim woman when you take your children to school. I'd encourage you to ask them for coffee or have a meal with them. If your children are the same age, even something like school-related topics can bring you together.

Perhaps you know of a practicing Muslim in your office or maybe even someone who is culturally Muslim but not involved in a local mosque. Think about the following scenario: you are attending an office party and you are sitting next to a Muslim coworker. How do you go about sharing your faith? How can you bring up faith without it becoming a wedge or a threat? Think about a good place to start, perhaps with family values, and see how it might lead to opportunities to better understand what he or she believes.

What would you like to see happen in America as evidence of bridge building between Christians and Muslims?

My wish is that Christians wouldn't shun Muslims because of the disappointing stories in the news and unrest in the Middle East. The truth is that they are here living in the United States. Most of us cannot go to Muslim countries; God has brought them here to us. If they turn away, then at least you've known they have heard the Gospel. I think it also helps to realize there are three major groupings of Muslims: Sunni, Sufi, and Shi'ite.

Sunni *means "tradition," and this group emphasizes following the traditions of Muhammad and the first two generations of Muslims. About 85 to 90 percent of all Muslims claim to be Sunni.*

Shi'ites make up about 10 percent of the population. They are known as the party of "Ali," who believe that that Muhammad's son-in-law, Ali, was his designated successor. Shi'ites and Sunnis have differing political views, so they most likely attend different mosques.

Sufi are Islamic mystics. Sufis go beyond external requirements to seek a personal experience with God through meditation and spiritual growth. One can be Sufi within a Sunni or Shi'ite sect.

Though you don't need to do an exhaustive study, the more you know about a Muslim worldview, the more equipped you will be.

What has been the hardest obstacle for you in building bridges?

When you begin to talk about Jesus, it is very hard for a Muslim to grasp the Trinity, because they feel there is one God—Allah. Muslims also struggle with embracing the idea that Jesus died—accepting Him as fully God means that God died.

I've found that encouraging Muslims to read the Gospel of Luke is a good place to begin. Luke shares a lot about the love of God and how Jesus related to people, how He came to heal the sick with power. If they can get the revelation of how much God loves them, it makes it much easier to see them become more and more curious about Jesus. Jesus' earthly ministry is not expounded upon in the Qu'ran, so they don't know about many of the healing miracles. I find this usually grabs their attention.

They say Allah and God are the same. But sometimes I ask the question, "Well if Allah is the same as God and the Qu'ran says to kill Christians and Jews, and if you leave Islam you will be killed, how can it be okay to kill those who have the "same" God? The Bible doesn't say if you leave Christianity would do that. When you ask them that, they tend to struggle to reconcile this.

How can we overcome the wounds of 9/11?

We need to love even those who seem to be our enemy. Jesus always expressed love for the lost. He says, "Pray for your enemies." This isn't just a suggestion but a command. If we pray for Muslims in our city, God can begin the healing process. Yes, we experienced an act of evil at the hands of terrorists. But God promises to heal the brokenhearted, so the answer is to turn to Him, to love and forgive, seventy times seven.

What stereotypes do Muslims have about Christians?

I think the most common assumption is that Christians don't like them. In fact, they often believe that Christians hate them. I don't think most of us hate Muslims; rather, I think I we believe most are terrorists, and that simply isn't true. They are tired of the stereotypes that Arabic names are names of terrorists. They tend to believe the media is biased against Muslims.

Do you find that most American Muslims are open to friendship?

Yes, I honestly do. I think of the Muslim family I've mentioned with the transportation business, who have all been in my home for meals and prayer. I've found Tara, their daughter, to be so receptive and warm. She has spent time in our home and going to church with us. I think she is hungry and seeking truth. She knows I genuinely love her and want to see her succeed.

What do you believe are the top five stereotypes that Americans hold toward Muslims?

1. *Muslims hate us.*
2. *Muslims are violent.*
3. *Muslims cannot fit into society.*
4. *Their lifestyle and beliefs are so different that we cannot bridge them.*

5. Muslims aren't open to Christianity and are too spiritually blinded.

I think about my friend Mani and his radical conversion. He of course considered himself to be an agnostic Muslim, not practicing or involved and connected to a mosque. His two friends reached out in genuine love and concern during a very difficult time in his life. He did convert and now is a pastor and evangelist.

What are some scriptures I can read that would help me to become a better neighbor?

John 3:16–17 is powerful and central. Jesus didn't come to condemn the world, but rather He came to save it. I like to point to any Scriptures that point to God's love for sinners. While we were yet sinners, Christ died for us (Romans 5:8).

When we were in Karachi, we had round-the-clock security. These young men were fully armed and, at a glance, very intimidating. But they were as friendly as can be. Many of them would stop us in our coming and going and ask, "Would you pray for me?" One of the young men called his aunt so I could pray for her over the phone. Some would ask for prayers of healing and if we would lay hands on them.

The most discouraging obstacle to this type of ministry is the doors that close so often. I want to have the opportunity to be a neighbor to all Muslim countries, but sometimes the timing is wrong and sometimes it feels like every attempt pushes us backward, not forward. We've tried to get into Syria and Algeria, but at times it looks impossible. Still we keep trying, keep persevering. And in my heart, I believe what is best for these Muslim countries is to come and pray for healing because they are so open to prayer.

I believe there are so many factors working against who God is. This issue—who God is—seems to be challenged more today than ever before. We have to know who God is, who we believe Him to be, before we can reach out in the confidence God desires us to have. Friendship has the ability to bless another soul, even when you disagree on most everything. God has ways of using diversity and revealing who He is when we grapple with our own faith against someone else's. I do believe a blessing awaits all those who are willing to reach out in love. It's worth the risk.

Conclusion

In 1987, the world heard President Reagan's liberating words: "General Secretary Gorbachev, if you seek peace, if you seek prosperity for the Soviet Union and Eastern Europe . . . open this gate! Mr. Gorbachev, tear down this wall!" Though the barbed wire, the dog runs, and some of the guarded check points were gone, the spirit of the Communist regime was still alive in Moscow. The Russian people were living in poor conditions, still starving, because of the belligerence of a government in need of reform. But in the midst of an impoverished country, it was a time in history when people were hungrier for God than for food. Many missionaries felt the call to go in, despite the cancelled venues, persecution, and economic hardship. I know of churches that are still standing due to the faith of those who believed they could get in and share the love of Christ with those who hadn't heard about Christianity.

I'm not sure the world ever thought the communist walls would come down, but they did. I'm not sure if Nehemiah, who felt the call of God to rebuild the Jerusalem walls, thought God would choose him to rebuild the city, brick by brick. My heart and my sights are on Iran. There are strongholds and walls that prevent the Gospel from coming into Iran, but I believe at the right time I may have the blessing of going in to share the healing power of Jesus. I don't know fully what it looks like, but I have a burden to go in. I've witnessed so many times before: God can open any door. He can tear down any wall and build a beautiful bridge. I know I can go in with His favor. His ways are higher. And His timing is how He shows His sovereignty. My job is to just know He is more than able to do more than I could ask think or imagine (Ephesians 3:20–21).

ACKNOWLEDGMENTS

Thank you to the following people:

Stephen Kiser for paving the way and running with the vision to open the doors to countries around the world and set up my international events.

Robinson Asghar for making it possible to reach the masses in Pakistan with Jesus' love.

Juana Vigil for accompanying me to Pakistan and bearing witness to God's love toward Muslims.

Jennifer Elahi for being a great blessing and a joy to know.

All my Muslim friends—through our inter-faith friendships you've confirmed that "I love Muslims and Muslims love me."

Live the Bible. Experience the Miracles.

Marilyn Hickey Ministries is sending a clear message of love, hope and healing to people around the world through Bible teaching, international healing meetings, group ministry tours, pastors' and leaders' conferences, humanitarian efforts, and the daily television program, *Today with Marilyn and Sarah*.

Whether Marilyn and Sarah are traveling domestically or internationally, they are seeing lives literally changed by God and His Word. Together with our partners:

- We've traveled to 126 countries, hosted 55 group tours, and held more than 40 International Meetings, with more every year
- In 2012, we held Pakistan's largest religious gathering ever: 400,000 attended, and thousands gave their lives to Christ
- We've sent tents, water, and blankets to Pakistani earthquake survivors
- We held healing meetings in Sudan: 200,000 attended, 40,000 responded to give their lives to Christ
- We built water wells in Ethiopia and bomb shelters in Sderot, Israel
- We funded a community center in Indonesia following the Tsunami
- We reach 130 countries though TV and media (with a potential audience of 2.2 billion households worldwide)

Marilyn and Sarah live out their great desire to help unite people. Where there is need, there is a call to respond. With true Christian humanitarian hearts, Marilyn, Sarah, and Marilyn Hickey Ministry partners have helped millions of individuals overcome setbacks and live the Bible.

The need has never been greater for the hope of the truth of God's love for His people. Thank you for caring enough to learn more about our work. Please visit our website.

www.marilynandsarah.org

dinner
·········· WITH ··········
Muhammad